GROWING
AS A LE

BCS, THE CHARTERED INSTITUTE FOR IT

BCS, The Chartered Institute for IT, is committed to making IT good for society. We use the power of our network to bring about positive, tangible change. We champion the global IT profession and the interests of individuals, engaged in that profession, for the benefit of all.

Exchanging IT expertise and knowledge

The Institute fosters links between experts from industry, academia and business to promote new thinking, education and knowledge sharing.

Supporting practitioners

Through continuing professional development and a series of respected IT qualifications, the Institute seeks to promote professional practice tuned to the demands of business. It provides practical support and information services to its members and volunteer communities around the world.

Setting standards and frameworks

The Institute collaborates with government, industry and relevant bodies to establish good working practices, codes of conduct, skills frameworks and common standards. It also offers a range of consultancy services to employers to help them adopt best practice.

Become a member

Over 70,000 people including students, teachers, professionals and practitioners enjoy the benefits of BCS membership. These include access to an international community, invitations to roster of local and national events, career development tools and a quarterly thought-leadership magazine. Visit www.bcs.org/membership to find out more.

Further Information
BCS, The Chartered Institute for IT,
First Floor, Block D,
North Star House, North Star Avenue,
Swindon, SN2 1FA, UK.
T +44 (0) 1793 417 424
(Monday to Friday, 09:00 to 17:00 UK time)
www.bcs.org/contact

http://shop.bcs.org/

GROWING YOURSELF AS A LEADER
Technical leadership capabilities

Brian Sutton and Robina Chatham

bcs
The Chartered Institute for IT

The right of Brian Sutton and Robina Chatham to be identified as authors of this work has been asserted by them in accordance with sections 77 and 78 of the Copyright, Designs and Patents Act 1988.

Published by BCS Learning & Development Ltd, a wholly owned subsidiary of BCS, The Chartered Institute for IT, First Floor, Block D, North Star House, North Star Avenue, Swindon, SN2 1FA, UK. www.bcs.org

ISBN: 978-1-78017-391-7
PDF ISBN: 978-1-78017-386-3
ePUB ISBN: 978-1-78017-387-0
Kindle ISBN: 978-1-78017-388-7

Ebook available

British Cataloguing in Publication Data.
A CIP catalogue record for this book is available at the British Library.

Disclaimer:

BCS books are available at special quantity discounts to use as premiums and sale promotions, or for use in corporate training programmes. Please visit our 'Contact us' page at www.bcs.org/contact

Publisher's acknowledgements

Reviewer: Daniel Breston
Publisher: Ian Borthwick
Commissioning Editor: Rebecca Youé
Production Manager: Florence Leroy
Project Manager: Sunrise Setting Ltd
Cover work: Alexander Wright
Picture credits: Shutterstock © Pavel Llyukhin

Typeset by Lapiz Digital Services, Chennai, India.
Printed and bound by Henry Ling Limited, at the Dorset Press, Dorchester, DT1 1HD

CONTENTS

LIST OF FIGURES

ABOUT THE AUTHORS

Professor Brian Sutton has over 40 years' management and leadership experience. He has developed comprehensive information systems (IS) strategies, conducted large-scale re-engineering initiatives and led major organisational change. He regularly contributes articles to professional journals and speaks at major professional gatherings. He holds a Doctorate in Corporate Education, a master's degree in Information Systems Management from the London School of Economics and has worked extensively in both the private and public sectors in Europe and the United States. He was formerly a Professor of Systems Management in the Information Resources Management College of the National Defense University in Washington DC. He is currently Professor of Learning Performance in the Faculty of Professional and Social Sciences at Middlesex University.

Dr Robina Chatham has over 35 years' experience in IT. She has held positions that range from IT project manager within the shipbuilding industry to European CIO for a leading merchant bank and lecturer at Cranfield School of Management. She is qualified as both a mechanical engineer and a neuroscientist. Previous books include *Corporate Politics for IT Managers: how to get streetwise*; *Changing the IT Leaders' Mindset: time for revolution rather than evolution*; and *The Art of IT Management: practical tools and techniques*. Robina now runs her own company specialising in management development and executive coaching. She is also a visiting fellow at Cranfield School of Management and a research associate for the Leading Edge Forum. Her prime focus is on helping senior IT managers to increase their personal impact and influence at board level.

FOREWORD

I am delighted to be able, in some small way, to contribute to this piece of work.

Robina and Brian are rare creatures, gathering together a lifetime of experience to help guide the next generation of leadership to achieve what they want to. Their mix of real-world experience, coupled with intellectual rigour and a passion for their subject is what makes this book a success.

I, personally, have found the structure of the book constantly engaging and it has encouraged me to think in entirely new ways about established topics.

Furthermore, its clear and simple focus on the idea of leadership being about a mindset rather than a set of skills to exercise is, for me, where its power really sits. In some respects, it turns the traditional notion of leadership on its head. In the place of control and skills development, the authors offer you the idea of creating a more positive environment where the freedom to perform has been granted.

Leadership, I think, is not really about achieving objectives and success for you and your teams. In my humble opinion, it's much bigger and more important than that. If you lead well, whether in your professional or private life, you fundamentally enrich the lives of everyone you touch. In the way that we can all name a teacher who inspired us and left an indelible mark on us, as leaders we have that same opportunity and responsibility.

In many ways leadership is an awesome responsibility and I feel it's an honour for us all to have been placed in that environment. I know I've found it endlessly fascinating, frustrating and rewarding in equal measure. But there has never been a dull day and for that I'm hugely grateful.

I hope this book inspires you and takes you on a rewarding journey. You're certainly in very good hands.

Simon La Fosse
Founder and Chairman of La Fosse Associates

ACKNOWLEDGEMENTS

We would like to offer our sincere thanks to all the people who have attended our training courses around the world. You have inspired and motivated us to produce this work; the shape and content of this book came about as a direct result of your questions. So, when we sat down to write this book, we did not ask ourselves, 'What do we know that we wish to tell other people?' Instead, we have built this book around your questions and the answers that you inspired in us, as we struggled to find the best ways of guiding you in your unique challenges. Without you, this book would never have seen the light of day.

To those of you who are familiar with our work, we hope that you will find renewed value in hearing again the ideas that we tried so hard to convey as we answered your questions. To those who are coming to us for the first time, we hope that some of the content will inspire you to see and be different, and to find new understanding in your working relationships.

Last, but by no means least, we need to say a huge thank you to our respective partners, Angela and John. They are a constant support, and without their patience and understanding we could never have completed this book.

PREFACE

ACKNOWLEDGEMENTS

Most people who find themselves in a leadership position for the first time are lost and unprepared. The challenge of stepping up to leadership is not something that can be overcome by attending a course or reading a book that abstractly talks about planning or motivation or delegation. There is a big difference between understanding the theory of how something works and being able to apply those ideas in practice, especially if things are going wrong and you are under pressure to get results.

We work extensively with mid- and senior-level leaders in the IT sector across national boundaries and cultures. We find common issues whether we are working with technical team leaders or the senior leadership team – they all ask us similar questions and they always start with the words 'How do I ...?'.

But we have come to realise that generally they are not asking for theory; they already have the knowledge of what to do. They just have no idea of how to go about doing it in their particular situation and circumstances.

When you engage with people as their leader, you are not simply directing work; you are engaged in creating and sustaining an environment within which they can deploy their various talents to collectively achieve great outcomes – outcomes that make a real difference in the lives of business partners, clients, customers and constituents.

Successful leaders realise that success comes more through their ability to create a positive environment where their staff feel valued, trusted and free to exercise their professional judgement than by constraining people to blindly follow existing processes.

Every situation that you face as a leader will have an element of uniqueness; every interaction will be coloured by the hopes, fears and aspirations of all parties. What makes leadership so difficult is that all too often you are unaware of your own driving forces, let alone those that drive the people you are leading.

When we are consulting with IT leaders at all levels we hear the same complaints – too much work, too few resources, too much change, conflicting priorities and customers who don't understand our problems. We see good people running faster just to stay in the same place and too many people facing 'burn out'. It need not be like this but it takes courage and focus from the leader to change the situation for everyone's benefit.

In this book, we look at six key aspects that we have come to believe are critical to an IT leader's ability to grow themselves both as a professional practitioner and as a person. The focus of this book is therefore on you, the individual; however, it is important to appreciate that personal growth is almost always achieved with the help of others and is often a catalyst and enabler for others to grow with you.

Key to personal growth is the understanding that you are neither defined nor limited by your current circumstances. The only limits on what you can achieve are the limits you place on yourself. Therefore, in Chapter 1, we start with personal mastery, what it is and what it takes to achieve mastery in any field of endeavour. Often we fail to achieve our own full potential because fear of failure stops us from trying something new or different. One area where we see this most is the self-limiting belief that you are not 'a creative type', as if creativity is something that only rare people are born with. The ability to exhibit creativity and release it in others is an important role of the leader, so in Chapter 2 we look at ways to unlock your own creative potential. By now you should be seeing a recurring pattern in our thinking: that learning and learning to learn is a critical skill for any leader. For this reason, in Chapter 3 we look at how you can develop yourself through mentoring and coaching others. In organisational terms this is a win–win situation, as you gain and the people you interact with also gain.

In any organisational setting you are not an island: you function within a rich and often messy web of organisational relationships. Your ability to bring about positive outcomes for your team and your organisation will largely depend on your ability to exercise influence at all levels within your organisation; therefore in Chapter 4 we look at ways of 'playing' the political game whilst maintaining a sense of personal integrity.

If you are successful in developing the skills and attitudes that we have identified in the first four chapters, the net result will be lots of new opportunities to bring about changes in your organisation that stem from new forms of individual and collective learning. As a leader, it is important that you are seen as someone who can achieve personal success whilst releasing and sustaining excellent levels of engagement and performance from all the members of your team. This is a fundamental aspect of leadership and it takes time, so the focus of Chapter 5 is on managing your time. In the final chapter, Chapter 6, we recognise that things do not always go as planned, mistakes are made, disasters happen. As a leader, it is important that you find the personal resilience to keep positive even when the odds appear to be stacked against you.

Each of the chapters follows the same structure. Each contains short anecdotes of how real people have applied some of this book's ideas. We point to resources for you to develop deeper engagement and understanding and we provide a series of simple things you can do now to start to develop into a more successful team leader.

Throughout the book you will see icons in the margin to focus your attention on particular aspects. Below you will find the key.

GOLDEN RULE

The golden rule to remember, even if you don't remember anything else about the chapter.

ANECDOTE

An anecdote or case study; real-life experience from leaders who have faced these situations and taken purposeful action.

KEY IDEA

Key ideas to unlock potential. Things you should be trying to build into your professional practice.

QUESTIONS TO ASK YOURSELF

Get into the habit of asking yourself these questions before you take action.

EXERCISE REGIMES

Things you can try immediately together with hints on how to adopt and adapt the ideas to your unique situation.

RESOURCES

Links to resources where you can find additional helpful and inspiring ideas.

We are always fascinated to hear of your experiences in applying the ideas we have presented. Please email us with examples from your personal experience and we will seek to include them in future editions of this book series.

Brian Sutton and Robina Chatham

drbriansutton@gmail.com
robina@chatham.uk.com

1 BUILDING PERSONAL MASTERY

The focus of this chapter is on techniques you can use to go beyond being just good at your job and become truly outstanding; to be all you can be. To achieve this, you will need to become much more deliberate in choosing and working on things you want to improve, and you will also need to tune your senses to acquire feedback from every possible source and then use this feedback as a learning mechanism. Through learning, you get better at what you do and you also develop the personal courage to strive to be great at things that you currently believe are beyond your ability.

WHY IS THIS IMPORTANT?

When we talk of personal mastery we are describing the process of developing true expertise in a field.

It is natural to aspire to be an expert, but in looking for role models people often look outside their profession for inspiration about how people achieve mastery. For example, when you look at top artists or sportsmen or sportswomen it is easy to think that such expertise is a step too far for you. In many cases that may be true to an extent, but it is not the whole story. Almost all top performers share the following common traits:

- They practise intensively and in a very focused and deliberate way. On average, the evidence appears to suggest that it takes about 10,000 hours of practice over a period of around 10 years to reach elite performance.[1]

- They study with devoted and talented teachers and coaches who are dedicated to developing people.
- They are encouraged and supported in their development by their family and friends.

Rather than be disillusioned or daunted by the sheer scale of effort put in by these role models, you should draw comfort from these statistics. These experts achieved brilliance through hard work and focused deliberate practice. If they can do it, so can you. But what is the difference between deliberate practice and the routine consolidation of your skills that you engage in every day of the week?

There is an old adage that says:

Practice makes perfect.

The reality is that practice just makes you better at doing what you are already doing and more certain that what you are doing is right. Without appropriate feedback and reflective thought, you can never hope to get truly better at doing anything.

Within the context of learning by doing in the workplace, you can think of the process in the following way; you take action, observe the results, reflect on why things turned out the way they did, and then you think about how you can modify your actions or approach next time to get different or better results.

This is termed the **learning loop** and was articulated neatly by David Kolb in 1983.[2] In order for you to learn, experience has to be backed up by reflection which, in turn, allows you to make generalisations and formulate concepts that can then be applied to new situations.

[1] Ericsson, K.A., Prietula, M.J. and Cokely, E.T. (2007) 'The making of an expert'. *Harvard Business Review.* Available from: https://hbr.org/2007/07/the-making-of-an-expert [20 November 2017].

[2] Kolb, D.A. (1983) *Experimental Learning: experience as the source of learning and development.* London: Prentice Hall.

The thing that makes Kolb's learning loop work is **feedback** – information that you receive from the real world that helps you understand how things are playing out. Feedback is a critical element for learning and growth.

> If you want to achieve personal mastery at anything, you need to look for feedback on your current performance and then reflect on what that feedback is telling you.

Everything you do is an opportunity to learn and grow, but unless you get feedback you will never be able to take full advantage of these precious learning opportunities.

THE IMPACT OF THE ISSUE

There is a world of difference between being busy and being productive. Our organisations are full of busy people, people running on autopilot as they repeat with little thought the same tasks in the same way. Often enjoyment and fulfilment drain away and all that is left is getting through another day without actually screwing up. It need not be like this: you do have a choice. You can spend your days reacting to things as they hit you; if you do this you will inevitably have a sense that the world is happening to you and is outside of your control. Or you can adopt a more creative mindset and seek to create the future you want by the choices and actions you take today and every day.

If you choose to take a hand in creating your own future you will need to, first of all, imagine what that future could be, in terms of:

- what it would look and feel like;
- what you would be able to achieve if you could make it real;
- what you would need to put in place in order to get there.

3

This is, in effect, building a personal vision. Your vision needs to be challenging; ideally it should appear to lie just outside your possible grasp and it should be something that is going to take significant and sustained effort to achieve. If you are not heading somewhere significant and exciting you will just drift – most of the people in the workplace today are drifting. Drifters seldom get promoted and are highly unlikely to get to do the exciting and interesting jobs. You need to be driven and you need to be driving relentlessly towards a goal.

Comparing your personal vision to the current reality will highlight the gaps – the things that you need to change or improve in order to make progress. Some of the skills and abilities you need will be new to you or will feel awkward or uncomfortable, whilst others may need a little polishing. The key is to be selective and focus on one thing at a time.

Expertise is realised as a result of lots of small but significant improvements to lots of seemingly insignificant things rather than one big improvement to one thing.

The reason that many people find it so difficult to improve in the workplace is because they do not have a vision that drives them to a new level. They don't know how to apply themselves in a way that can yield results. They often don't have someone to inspire, guide and sustain them in their quest for excellence and mastery and, critically, they expect results too soon. The problem with shooting for the stars is that at the first setback it is tempting to give up or lower the goal, to say: 'Well, that was unrealistic. Perhaps I ought to attempt something a little less challenging.' Never give up or lower your goals. You may not achieve them all but the people who you admire and who succeed are the sorts of people who will strive relentlessly to achieve their goal. For them, failure is not an option.

If you fail to achieve your goal, don't lower it – change your approach to achieving it.

Once you start to work on improving your skills you will need a means to assess the progress that you are making. This normally comes in the form of feedback. You know from the last section that feedback is important, but, sadly, feedback is not always easy to come by.

Feedback comes in many forms: it can be tangible metrics of performance gathered as part of your business systems, or it can be more subjective assessments about how people are making sense of, and reacting to, the changes you have instituted. Feedback can be generic in terms of the contribution that your efforts have made or it can be more personal, about how you are perceived and reacted to as an individual. All types and styles of feedback are important and you need to reflect upon what the feedback tells you about both what you do and how you engage with people in order to do it.

Often the consequences of your decisions or actions do not show up until weeks, or even months, later. The outcomes, when they finally arise, do so all too often somewhere else along the value chain and, therefore, are not visible to you.

This causes a big problem in your feedback loop and it shows itself as follows:

- You meet an issue. Your brain recognises a pattern in the events and says, 'Oh, this is one of **them**'. If you have met the situation before, you are likely to remember what you did last time.

- You probably think that you did the right thing last time or in a similar situation and the obvious conclusion is that you didn't do it well enough, or that you should have done it faster or more vigorously.

- So, you do the same thing again, but with more vigour and certainty. The consequence is that you repeat solutions that fail and in many cases you keep repeating them ad infinitum because you never get feedback on the outcome, or consequences, of your actions.

This scenario is just as likely to show up in the way you handle your relationships as it is in the way you play out your organisational responsibilities. Day after day, you do what you always did; you always get the same results; you don't question those results, or witness the outcomes; and you don't take personal responsibility for those outcomes.

The result is that your leaders shake their heads in dismay and wonder why the same problems keep cropping up time after time, and why the competition appears to be more nimble and more innovative.

> You don't need to get better at what you are doing; you need to get better at understanding why you are doing what you are doing and recognising when you need to start doing something different.

MAKING SENSE OF IT ALL

In his book *The Fifth Discipline*,[3] Peter Senge identified personal mastery as an underpinning principle of organisational learning. According to Senge, to achieve personal mastery you must first set a personal vision: what you want to achieve and why this is important to you. This will then lead to what he terms 'creative tension': the feelings and impulses that arise in the space between where you want to be and the current reality. Without this creative tension, you are unlikely to summon the desire and achieve the sustained levels of effort needed to bring about a change in your personal circumstances.

Senge goes on to stress the importance of being loyal to the truth; this is a more difficult and contentious notion, not least because often our version of the truth is tied up with our assumptions about how the world works. We would suggest

---

[3] Senge, P.M. (1994) *The Fifth Discipline Fieldbook: strategies and tools for building a learning organization.* New York; London: Currency, Doubleday.

that at this stage of your development as a team leader it is possibly better to think in terms of integrity and by that we mean having a strong moral compass and being true to your beliefs and principles.

The starting point is personal vision: a desire to achieve something tangible, something that will stretch you, involving the acquisition of new skills, knowledge and habits. Your vision should be something that is capable of shifting the tectonic plates of your life and shaping you as a new and better person with new capabilities and horizons. The actual vision itself is far less important than what the vision does for you, how it triggers and sustains progress towards a new you.

The following mini case study helps to put this issue into context. Interestingly this story of personal transformation started more by accident than purposeful visioning, but the vision emerged as the story unfolded and the results were life changing.

Anne was a middle manager in the operations department of a large FMCG (fast-moving consumer goods) organisation. Anne was bright, hard-working, highly professional and well respected by her peers. She ran her department well and could be relied upon to do what was right and deliver a great quality service.

Anne came to the attention of the HR department and was offered the opportunity of a one-year sabbatical to go back to university and do a master's degree, paid for by the organisation. She was excited by the prospect and prepared herself for the challenge. Just a couple of weeks into the course, Anne realised that the key was not to learn new stuff, but rather to learn new ways of looking at stuff. She had to examine everything she knew and question why she thought about things the way that she did.

> With this new sense of 'self' came the crushing realisation that she did not have 15 years' experience of management – what she had was one year's experience repeated 15 times. Eventually, she came out of the programme knowing new things, seeing all things differently, and having a new sense of her own value and a commitment always to try to see everything as if for the first time.

Anne's story illustrates nicely that, paradoxically, personal mastery does not necessarily come from striving to perfect what you currently know and do. Anne's breakthrough came when she realised that the big pay-off came when she challenged herself to see and do new things; learning how to learn better and, crucially, realising that what was already in her head limited what she focused her attention on. To really learn differently you need to acquire the ability to see (perceive) differently.

> Sometimes the real clarity of a situation can only be seen when you view it from another perspective.

Personal mastery and development comes through discovering new ways of learning and embedding the desire to learn in everything that you do; learning is kick-started by new experiences.

So, the way to really get better is by grappling with things you don't know. You need to challenge what you think you know and how you came to be so certain about it. You need to spend more than half of your available time striving, however imperfectly, to seize the unknown.

At the end of each week ask yourself the question – 'What have I got better at this week that moves me towards the achievement of my goal?'

People who make significant improvements in their personal performance do so as a result of **deliberate practice**.

Most of the time when we choose to make the effort of practising something, we quickly fall into the habit of practising the things we can already do; after all, this feels good and gives us an instant psychological reward. But the research[4] shows that the route to expertise lies in practising the things that you can't do or that you find difficult.

To improve your performance you need to identify something specific that you either don't know how to do or that you are poor at and then work on that one thing in a sustained way. Once you have perfected that one thing you can then add it into your wider practice and look for the next small thing to work on.

In addition to physical activity, try to be deliberate in the thinking that is associated with the physical acts. Try talking through your strategy out loud before you take action; this all helps bring additional focus to your physical acts.

You may also benefit from consciously scheduling what time of day you tackle certain sorts of problems. Listen to your body clock and set time for your most difficult and mentally challenging deliberate practice when you are at your freshest and your best; for most people this will be at the start of the day.

The following story illustrates how, with a little thought, imagination and forward planning you can build deliberate practice into any situation.

---

[4] Ericsson, K.A., Prietula, M.J. and Cokely, E.T. (2007) 'The making of an expert'. *Harvard Business Review*. Available from: https://hbr.org/2007/07/the-making-of-an-expert [20 November 2017].

Tim was a web development team leader. A key element of his job was to accompany senior sales execs as they pitched for business to important clients. Tim was generally acknowledged as the most promising web developer in the company, but he was uncomfortable in the presence of the extrovert sales guys and was often marginalised or talked over in these important meetings. To make matters worse, Tim's boss was a charismatic personality who delivered knock-out sales presentations, answered client questions with authority and panache and was loved by all the sales team. Unless Tim could get better and win the trust of the sales team in the same way, he would never have a hope of stepping into his boss's shoes when his boss moved on.

Tim got on well with his boss and so asked him if he would mentor him. They adopted the following strategy.

A couple of days before an important sales pitch was to be delivered by his boss they would sit down and brainstorm all the key client needs and expectations and the unique ways in which their solution would fulfil these needs. They compiled a list of all the possible questions the client might have and the objections they might offer about the proposed solution. Tim would then go away independently and work up a slide pack and a persuasive response to all the questions. He would not share this with his boss.

On the day of the sales pitch, Tim would accompany his boss and sit at the back of the room – he would compare his boss's slide pack to his own and notice how his boss responded to questions from the floor. He made extensive notes on his own slide pack and briefing notes to show where their two approaches diverged and which elements of his boss's pitch had the most impact on the audience in terms of nodding and supportive comments. A couple of days after the event the two would sit down again and review what Tim had learned from the process and his boss would explain, where necessary, why he had made the choices he did. Together they would agree on one core aspect that should be the focus of their next mentoring session. This continued at least twice a month for 18 months.

Two years later the sales team no longer looked at Tim as technically capable but dull – he was now charismatic Tim who could be relied upon to wow clients. Three years later he moved up into his boss's job.

Tim's story highlights some key points. Getting better at something takes a lot of hard work and time. But effort on its own is not sufficient: Tim could not have achieved his transformation without the dedicated and selfless support of his boss. We all need support, encouragement and targeted feedback if we are to progress and achieve mastery at anything.

We have seen that to get the most benefit from your practice periods you need expert feedback, so you need to find a good coach, someone you trust and respect, someone who has real proven ability in the field you wish to excel in and someone who will both inspire and challenge you. One coach does not fit all purposes. As you grow and develop you will need different things from different people; your need may become for a mentor rather than a coach, for example.[5] Your coach or mentor will need to be skilled at giving feedback.

Feedback needs to be considered, targeted and balanced: too much feedback in general can be confusing and too much negative feedback in particular will be demoralising. The best

---

[5] Coaching is about personal effectiveness, growth and career development. It focuses on the achievement of specific goals or the resolution of certain performance or motivational issues. The role of a coach is to ask really good questions that make you think and motivate you to learn and do things differently. Coaching helps individuals access what they already know. They may never have asked themselves the questions but they have the answers. A coach assists, supports and encourages individuals to find these answers. Coaching is about helping people to learn rather than teaching them.

Mentoring is concerned with the passing on of knowledge or experience to someone less experienced or less qualified. Mentors may also open doors, act as sounding boards, or provide guidance, affirmation or reassurance to their 'mentee'.

coaches and mentors don't just focus on the here and now – they look forward and identify the skills and attitudes that you don't possess now but will need to develop in order to achieve your next goal.

> Great coaches and mentors will help you to develop your inner coach, so that you can become sensitive to your own performance in any situation and hence learn to self-coach.

The key to learning to self-coach is acquiring the ability to observe yourself, as a third party would, whilst you are engaged in your practice. This is not an easy skill. Most people, much of the time, will fall into one of two states: they will either be in the flow, so immersed in what they are doing that they are oblivious to the outside world, or they will be purposefully standing back from the action and consciously thinking about what they are experiencing and what they plan to do next. The second of these states is often termed 'reflecting on action', a term coined by Donald Schön in his landmark book *The Reflective Practitioner*,[6] and is an important skill to master. This sort of reflection is more than just noticing what is going on; it is also about asking yourself why you see and experience things in the way that you do. If you adopted a different perspective would you notice things differently in the same situation?

You will know that you are starting to become really effective as a self-coach when you are able to slip seamlessly and unconsciously between the two states – of flow and reflecting in the moment on the action you are taking. Schön termed this 'reflecting in action'. The bedrock of all coaching is asking powerful questions. As a self-coach, you will need to ask yourself reflective questions such as the following:

• What specific technique or skill have I been deliberately practising this week?

---

[6] Schön, D.A. (1991) *The Reflective Practitioner: how professionals think in action.* Aldershot: Arena.

- How much have I closed the gap between where this element of my practice is and where I want it to be?

- What has been the most rewarding outcome of this particular phase of practice and why?

- What has been the most frustrating thing about this phase of practice and why?

- What does the frustration I have felt tell me about how I should structure the next phase of my practice and what key learning target I should build into my performance vision?

The only way you will grow as a leader is by stretching the limits of who you are, and doing things that may make you uncomfortable but that teach you, through direct experience and feedback, who you want to become. Indeed, the moments that challenge your sense of self are the ones that teach you the most.

PRACTICAL ADVICE

We will split our advice into two parts:

1. getting better and achieving mastery in what you are currently doing;
2. getting better at learning, so that you can achieve mastery in something new.

First some tips on how to become a superstar at what you are currently doing.

- Set yourself performance goals for all the important things that you have to do. These goals should not be process goals; they need to be outcome focused. It is not good enough to do something faster if the end customer sees no benefit that is meaningful to them as a result of your efforts.

- Monitor your own success rate against your personal performance goals. What is your personal best?

- Get into the habit of visualising what it would feel like to set a new personal best:
  - How would you need to prepare differently?
  - What new skills or knowledge would you need?
  - How would you deploy your new-found skills and knowledge to do something that someone cares about differently in a way that produces a significantly different outcome or customer experience?
  - How will you know when you have achieved something new?
- Ask yourself how others would assess your performance. Ask people for feedback on the following indicators:
  - What is it like to work with you?
  - How do you make people feel?
  - What is the most significant contribution that people associate with you?
  - What do others see as your core strength?
  - What one or two things would others really like to change about how you do what you do?

Now turn your attention to doing things differently and also to doing different things.

In terms of doing things differently, our message is a simple one: every hour spent on up-front thinking and reflecting with an enquiring mind will pay big dividends and could save you 100 hours down the road, mopping up the consequential issues of a bodged job, or dealing with the quick fix when it fails. This up-front hour should be spent in the following way:

- Considering alternative approaches.
- Putting yourself in the shoes of the person, or people, who will receive the output of your efforts. Ask yourself what is important to them and how they would want you to improve what you are doing.

- Asking yourself if this will fix things in such a way that they are likely to stay fixed.

- Thinking how what you are doing is going to make things easier for your customer (by easier, we mean reducing the effort the customer has to expend in order to engage with you or your services).

- Ensuring that you are addressing the root cause of an issue rather than merely the symptoms.

- Considering what leadership style or tactics you could borrow from others, for example shaping opinion without being overbearing, or using humour to break tension.

You also need to find every opportunity you can to do something different. Our basic rule of thumb is that when looking for a new challenge you should try to aim for something that is 50 per cent familiar and 50 per cent completely unknown. You need the 50 per cent familiarity, or you are likely to freeze and become unable to act. The 50 per cent unknown forces you to think new things and imagine new solutions.

When you approach a new challenge, start by asking yourself these questions:

- What is different or new about this situation, problem or request? Then look for new angles.

- What are the big assumptions that underpin your thinking about this situation? Are those assumptions still valid?

- If you were coming at this for the first time with no prior knowledge, how would you react?

- What would be the first thing that made an impression on you?

- What would world-class performance on this issue look and feel like?

- How far are you away from providing world-class service?

- What is the single biggest barrier to success?

- What don't you know about this situation? Is the lack of that knowledge a roadblock that will stop progress or merely a speed bump that will slow you down?

- If you are facing a roadblock, can you find someone else who has the knowledge you need?

You also need to adopt a rigorous approach to creating opportunities to be different. We suggest that, at the start of each week, you choose one event that you may be called upon to repeat a number of times; for example, chairing a meeting, meeting a customer, or, maybe, briefing a team member on a task.

Then pick one aspect of the task; for example, planning for the task itself, how you use questions to steer the meeting, how you build rapport or how you check on understanding.

Whatever you decide to focus on, make sure that you do the following things:

- Be conscious of the thing you are trying to practise.

- Monitor your own feelings and internal struggles as you carry out your task.

- Monitor the reaction and behaviour of the people you are dealing with:

  - Were they at ease and receptive?

  - Were they following your train of thought?

  - Could they feed back to you an understanding of what you wanted?

  - Had you engaged both their hearts and minds, or just one aspect?

  - Did you get the level of contribution from them that you had hoped for?

  - Did anyone leave the room not understanding what you were aiming for or feeling that they did not have the opportunity to express their concerns, hopes and desires?

Now think about the outcomes you were hoping to achieve, and use those outcomes as feedback to guide your learning about the effectiveness of your new strategy:

- How confident and natural did you feel as you used the technique?
- What went really well?
- What could have gone better?
- What one or two things that you did appeared to resonate with the people you were working with? What got them excited?
- Did the energy you created produce a positive result?
- If you could immediately repeat the same exercise with the same people, what would you do differently and why?

Keep a reflective journal of what you tried, and what you observed happening as a result of what you tried. Capture how you felt, as well as what you did. In your reflective section focus on:

- what you learned from the events of the day or week;
- what you might have done differently if you had been able to view the same events from a different perspective.

At the end of each week review your learning and try to identify:

- two things that you will try to do more of;
- two things that you will try to do less of.

Achieving personal mastery is all about:

1. setting a goal and putting in time and effort to achieve it;
2. finding ways of getting feedback on your progress;
3. reflecting on what the feedback tells you about yourself and your impact, in the context of your goal;
4. using your new understanding to modify what you do and how you think going forward.

The process that we have described above looks pretty straightforward but, in our experience, the facet that people have most difficulty with is reflection. Our advice would be to get yourself a coach or trusted adviser. It is important to understand that, when choosing a coach, you are not looking for someone who can tell you what to do. You are looking for someone who can listen to your experiences and then ask you really good questions, questions that make you think and that kick-start your learning process.

> The key to achieving personal mastery in anything is reflection and learning, and having the courage to try something new.

If you want to achieve mastery in everything you do, you have to find learning opportunities in everything that you do.

By all means take pride in doing something well, but always remain alert to the possibility that maybe you could have done it even better. It is the quest for continuous improvement that marks out the star performers.

THINGS FOR YOU TO WORK ON NOW

Below are some questions that will help you build a picture of how you currently seek and value feedback about your own performance and contribution to significant outcomes.

KEY QUESTIONS TO ASK YOURSELF

- How do I judge and measure my own performance?
- How much of my time does fire-fighting and rework consume?
- When did I last actively seek feedback about how my efforts contribute to achieving outcomes that are meaningful to our customers?

- When did I last seek feedback about how my style of engagement impacts or inhibits the achievement of key goals?

- Have my stories, my defining moments or my self-image become outdated?

- How often do I challenge myself to think and see things in a different way and then reflect upon how I could do things differently?

- How concerned am I about how I appear, and how afraid am I to take risks in the service of learning?

- When I look at people in the organisation who are considered to be star performers, what are the key things about how they operate that are different to my way of behaving that I feel I could emulate?

Reflect on your answers to these questions. Decide on whether you wish to work on perfecting a current personal practice or embark on achieving mastery at something new, then choose one of the techniques we identified on pages 13 to 17 and use those ideas to help you tackle the mini exercises below.

MINI EXERCISES YOU CAN TRY IMMEDIATELY

- Start to keep a personal diary of learning – jot down things that you do that work well and things that don't work quite so well. How did you recognise that they were working, or not working?

- Set aside some quiet time to review your learning diary and reflect on how you can change one or two of the things you do. Make a plan of how you will change those things and be rigorous about following through on your planned actions.

- Ask for feedback from your staff, your boss, your peers and your customers. Ask them what they value most about your style and approach and what they value least.

- Get yourself a mentor or coach and be prepared to have at least two sessions in the first month and then at least one session per month for a minimum of a year.

- Set yourself three personal performance goals. How will you measure your progress and how will you know when you have achieved these goals?

- Understand that you can also improve performance by eliminating some behaviours – identify two things that you are currently doing that are getting in the way of improved performance and vow to stop doing them. Once you have succeeded with these two, set yourself another two.

If you are inspired to find out more about any of the themes covered in this chapter we suggest that you start by reviewing the resources listed below.

FURTHER FOOD FOR THE CURIOUS

- Ericsson, K.A., Prietula, M.J. and Cokely, E.T. (2007) 'The making of an expert'. *Harvard Business Review*. Available from: https://hbr.org/2007/07/the-making-of-an-expert [20 November 2017].

  - A short 15-page paper with lots of inspiring and fascinating examples.

- Goleman. D. (1995) *Emotional Intelligence*. New York: Bantam Books.

  - A comprehensive text on the subject of emotional intelligence. One of the five emotional intelligences that Goleman describes is 'motivating yourself to achieve peak performance'.

- Schön, D.A. (1991) *The Reflective Practitioner: how professionals think in action*. Aldershot: Arena.

  - A must-read for the more thoughtful professional who is committed to learning and self-coaching.

- Senge, P.M. (1994) *The Fifth Discipline Fieldbook: strategies and tools for building a learning organization*. New York; London: Currency, Doubleday.

  - The classic text on the elements of building a learning organisation. This is an easier read than the original book, *The fifth discipline* (1990), and is set out in a very accessible way with lots of clear examples. Dip in to sample a specific idea.

- Taylor, D. (2002) *The Naked Leader*. Oxford: Capstone.

  - An easy read with many poignant truths and practical tips.

2 UNLOCKING YOUR OWN CREATIVE POTENTIAL

The focus of this chapter is on your ability to imagine and deliver against your goals in ways that delight and surprise, and mark you out as someone who creates amazing results. One of the key questions at any job interview is: 'Give me an example of how you came up with a new and creative solution in the last six months.' Many organisations clearly want and value creative people; but is creative ability something you are born with or is it something you can nurture and develop?

WHY IS THIS IMPORTANT?

In the 1990s, the business mantra was that the only sustainable source of competitive advantage was knowledge. It was this belief that gave rise to knowledge management as organisations strove to collect, identify, classify, create and share knowledge that could drive and transform their business processes. Nowadays the focus has subtly changed; if you want to stay competitive you must continuously innovate. But, crucially, innovation is no longer seen as being just about new product development; innovation is also the key to the redesign of services, management practices and, most importantly, customer experience. The focus on innovation has opened up new thinking about the design process and the role of creativity. It also puts a premium on access to creative talent and connecting people together in a more holistic way to foster innovation.

Creativity is associated with originality of thought, or inventiveness.

Whenever you interact with a representative of an organisation, whether the receptionist at a hotel, your IT helpdesk or a sales representative from another company, you probably would like them to show a little imagination in the way they deal with you.

What you want them to understand is that you are an individual with unique needs and that their role is not to make you fit their preferred process or product, but rather to seek to understand your needs and then use their imagination and creativity to tailor their product or service to fulfil them.

What you do not want is to be forced to conform to a one-size-fits-all approach. You want your own particular size, and you want it delivered in a way that satisfies your need or desired outcome.

Your customers want the same thing from you.

THE IMPACT OF THE ISSUE

How often do you feel frustrated, or even angry, at the service, or lack of service, that you receive? When you hear the words 'No, you can't have that', or 'We only serve that after 11 a.m.', or 'That's not our policy', and so on, what is your reaction? What you want is a positive, 'can do' attitude; you want to hear what can be done, rather than what can't be done; you want people to think outside of the box and offer you alternatives and options; what you don't want is bureaucracy, red tape and rules just for the sake of them.

First and foremost you want someone to empathise with your situation, you want to be made to feel that the person you are dealing with is on your side and they will go that 'extra mile' to try to resolve your problem. Often front-line support staff won't have all the relevant knowledge or information to solve your problem immediately, but they need to give you the confidence that they will come back to you and be proactive and stay on the case until the problem has been resolved to your satisfaction. Inevitably this will require the service-giver to exercise a little creativity.

> It is not enough to simply experience a slick and efficient
> process – people also want to see imagination, flair and
> creativity that make them feel special and good about
> what they are getting.

What you want from others you should also strive to deliver
yourself. There is also the added bonus that when you are
creative, you almost always feel more fulfilled.

MAKING SENSE OF IT ALL

Whilst not all of us can aspire to the intuitive ability of some
of the great chief executives who can turn a company around
overnight, you can maximise your own creative potential by
opening your mind and harnessing the collective abilities of
those around you.

Some people are naturally ideas-oriented, whilst others are
more practical in their approach. Ideas people tend to be more
imaginative. For them, ideas come frequently and those ideas
do not have to be either practical or realistic; it is volume that
counts. Practical people, on the other hand, instinctively go into
evaluation mode and can spot that one good idea out of 100
and bring it to fruition; for them it's quality that counts.

The process of bringing a new product, service or experience
to market, for example, requires both types of thinking and
both sets of abilities, as illustrated by the model in Figure 2.1.

Such a process requires collaboration among different types of
people; people who see the world in inherently different ways.
They need to work together constructively and creatively; in
order to do this, they must value and respect each other's skills
and talents. However, all too often, such differences in style
and approach result in unproductive conflict among people
who do not innately understand or value one another. Disputes
become personal and, as a consequence, the symbiosis of the
creative–innovative processes breaks down.

Figure 2.1 Creativity–innovation processes

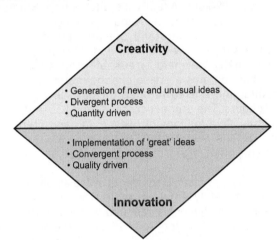

To be creative, you must first be open to the idea that things could be different and that, often, what may appear at the outset to be a great solution is, in effect, just a convenient one.

To be innovative, you must be brave enough to challenge convention, the status quo and accepted wisdom; to have the courage and conviction to run with that novel or unusual idea.

Consider the following mini cases.

Each year around 20 million premature babies are born worldwide and over 4 million of these will die. The issue is that these babies don't have the fat reserves to regulate their own body temperature; in a hospital environment they would be placed in an incubator and they would have a good chance of survival. But in the developing world most babies are born at home far from the nearest hospital and have no access to sophisticated incubators that typically cost around £20,000. A team of students from Stanford University spent time in Nepal working with local communities to understand the problem and came up with a simple, low-cost solution. The result is the Embrace baby warmer, a reusable and sterilisable pouch that contains a phase change material capable of maintaining a fixed temperature for between four and six hours. The product costs around £50 and could potentially save millions of lives. If you are interested in the details watch the TED talk: www.ted.com/talks/jane_chen_a_warm_embrace_that_saves_lives

Another group of technicians came at the same problem from a completely different angle. They realised that even when aid agencies donated expensive Western equipment like incubators to hospitals in the developing world, many were used for a short while and then ended up in a storeroom. The problem was lack of parts and the ability to maintain the equipment; key components were frequently burned out due to fluctuating power supplies. The technicians' solution took a different creative path – they asked what parts were plentiful in rural areas of the developing world and what repair skills local people possessed. The answer was scrap car parts and the ability to get beaten-up cars working again. The solution therefore became the NeoNurture car parts incubator that uses headlamps as a heat source and car air filters and fans to govern airflow. To learn more about this approach check out https://wheels.blogs.nytimes.com/2010/11/23/neonurtures-car-parts-baby-incubator/

These two stories tell us a number of things about creativity. The first important point is that both groups found their route to creativity by deeply immersing themselves in the 'lived experience' of the community they were trying to serve. The immersion was not a brief foray; they needed to experience for themselves the operational environment. This deep immersion allowed them to:

- ask gentle, probing questions to get to the 'nub' of the issue, the root cause of the problem as experienced by the local community;

- actively listen and feel with all their senses without making judgement, or being critical;

- focus on the real issue in the moment, rather than ill-informed hearsay, incomplete information or second-hand guesswork about what might happen;

- test ideas in the moment, rapidly iterate around potential solutions, quickly find out what does not work and what does not meet needs, even if it does work, and move on until they found out what would both work and meet needs;

- collaborate with the local people to find a solution that really worked for them.

> You get more creative when you get out of the office and into the real world of people who use your products and services.

The second key lesson from the two stories is that success did not come quickly or without many small setbacks along the way. Experimentation started immediately and continued iteratively as the groups learned from successive failures. The experiments did not take place in a sterile environment back at the office or laboratory; they took place in the community under the scrutiny of the people who would benefit from the result. These were both very open and very collaborative acts of creativity.

> You cannot be creative unless you embrace and welcome failure as an opportunity to learn.

These two stories also demonstrate that creativity, in most organisational contexts, is not about being a naturally gifted genius, but rather about being willing to live in the world with the people who are on the receiving end of your products and services; ask probing questions and actively listen with all your senses. Then to quickly take small steps, learn from the experience, and then take more small steps whilst embracing failure as part of the process and being prepared to constantly challenge the status quo and accepted way of doing things.

David Kelly of Stanford University School believes that all humans are naturally creative, but that our creativity is stifled by our educational and organisational experience.[1] In life, people experience constant put-downs; you no doubt will have been told from an early age that you can't do certain things or, at times, that what you produced was rubbish. Over time, your beliefs can become self-limiting factors and your doubts get in the way of you becoming more than you are. Kelly listed the following four fears that he sees all the time in organisational contexts:

1. Fear of the messy unknown.
2. Fear of being judged (by others or by yourself).
3. Fear of the first step.
4. Fear of losing control.

Consider this personal tale:

Brian (one of the authors) started his professional life as an engineering draughtsman. This was in the days before computer-aided design (CAD) packages and involved working with paper and pencil. Over a period of several years, Brian gained considerable skill as an illustrator understanding perspective and three-dimensional images.

---

[1] Kelly, T. and Kelly, D. (2015) *Creative Confidence: unleashing the creative potential within us all.* London: William Collins.

He found that although he worked mostly with straight lines he could actually produce pretty good freehand sketches of people or urban scenes. One evening Brian joined his wife in her weekly art group. Everyone sat around splashing paint on the paper with gay abandon whilst Brian carefully used his pencil to produce an image of the local village street; after 45 minutes he had a picture he was truly proud of. Others gathered around and wondered why there was such detailed pencil work and when he was going to start painting and adding colour. Brian had no experience of mixing paints and within minutes of picking up a brush had ruined his fine drawing. Some 40 years on, Brian has never again picked up a paintbrush. No one criticised him but Brian was crushed by his own inner demons. He judged himself to have failed and this was compounded by a fear of taking the first step and of losing control.

Brian's story illustrates some important points. You saw in Chapter 1 that you build expertise through deliberate practice, by focusing on things you cannot do rather than on things you can do. Instead of throwing himself into the new and scary experience of splashing about with paint, Brian chose to practise what he could already do, namely draw. He did so because he wanted to experience success, to demonstrate his prowess at drawing. But this was a painting group. In focusing on what he could already do, he was just putting off the time when he would experience failure and he was guaranteeing that failure, when it came, would be even more crushing. The moral is:

Creativity is released when you start small, fail small and fail often.

Creativity is not something that is only possessed by a few amazing arty people. We are all creative but, like anything else, it is a skill that grows through deliberate practice. You need to give yourself permission to try and, since you know that you will experience failure, your practice regime should start with simple small steps. Build slowly from one step to the next as you experience mini moments of success.

This leads us to a further question – do modern times with issues of safety, the advent of technology and the abundance of instant entertainment also stifle our natural creativity? Children are naturally curious and creative, but the modern world encourages parents to keep their children safe, indoors watching the TV or absorbed in a computer game or on organised outings accompanied by adults.

Consider this second personal tale:

Robina (the other author) grew up in the 1950s. Then, the only regular source of laid-on entertainment was the Saturday Morning Pictures. Television was still for the minority and children's programmes were few and far between; computers were for atomic scientists. As a child in the 1950s, her friends and her imagination were the prime source of entertainment. She had a lot of freedom in comparison to the kids of today, and the excitement of games relied to a greater or lesser degree on the bounds of her imagination. She built dens and tree houses out of pieces of wood and scrap metal that she found lying around; she played cowboys and Indians with wooden spoons for guns and tree branches for arrows; when she was hungry she went scrumping for apples.

As Robina's story suggests, creativity comes when you unleash that inner child and free abandon. Let go of those fears and constraints you have learned over time; experience, experiment and imagine.

You unlock your creative side by letting go of the fears and constraints that trap you where you are.

PRACTICAL ADVICE

We have seen that creativity is released when you engage your inner child, park your fears, do not limit yourself by past experiences and engage openly with communities who you care about and are impacted by what you are working on. Creativity is essentially a learning process, and learning flourishes where there is openness; diversity of opinion, experience and attitude; safety to express and act without fear of judgement; and time to reflect and process what you are experiencing. All of these things are multiplied by the opportunity to build and create new things, whether physical artefacts, a new app or an enhanced service offering that tests your ideas in context. Creativity is not just an intellectual process; it has a strong 'right brained' component. Therefore we recommend that you make space for and work on developing the following aspects of yourself:

- your emotional intelligence:
  - understanding yourself, your style, values, strengths and weaknesses, behaviour, image and reputation;
  - understanding others, valuing and appreciating differences;
  - demonstrating empathy for others and being able to put yourself in their shoes and appreciate their perspective;
  - knowing what you want to achieve and having the drive and determination to get there and to cope with the inevitable setbacks;
  - keeping positive and optimistic even in the face of adversity;
  - building rapport, questioning and actively listening, and building upon the ideas and thoughts of others;
- your intuition:
  - the ability to detect patterns, or make connections that have not been made before, that others have overlooked or mistaken for random noise;

- listening to your subconscious – drawing on rules and patterns that you can't quite articulate;
- the ability to spot opportunities and see new possibilities;

- your curiosity:
  - being inquisitive, seeking out new knowledge and understanding and bringing those ideas from the outside into your organisation;
  - cultivating an openness to new experiences and a desire to try things out and experiment;
  - getting excited about the novel and the different, the weird and the wacky;
  - challenging the status quo and the accepted way of doing things.

Because the focus of this chapter is on increasing personal creativity, we will concentrate our advice on the creative, divergent phase of identifying ideas and possibilities rather than on the innovative, convergent phase of narrowing down the possibilities and homing in on a course of action, as illustrated in Figure 2.1.

When in creative mode, it is important to remember the following key rules:

- Begin with an easily understandable goal statement. A statement beginning with 'To ...', which is no more than 12 words in length and written in plain English.

- Remember that anything and everything goes. Every idea is written down. The objective is to capture as many ideas as possible; the wackier, the better. No idea should be critiqued, judged or discarded during the creative process. Don't aim to produce 10 ideas – aim for 100.

- Use building, encouraging words, such as '**and**', rather than condemning or closing words, such as '**but**'. Spark off and build upon the ideas of others; think laterally.

- Take sufficient time – there is evidence[2] that ideas seem to peak and decline, and then spring back to life again, as illustrated in Figure 2.2.

Figure 2.2 Ideas timeline

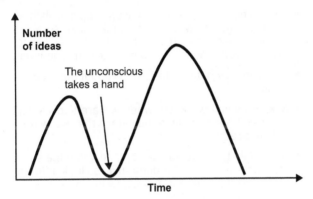

- The key insight from Figure 2.2 is that most of the time most people will close down on idea generation before they get into the second phase of creativity. So, the question you need to be asking is, 'Have we run out of ideas because we have exhausted all possibilities or have we stopped because our unconscious mind is having a rest?' Here are a few things that you can try to jump-start the ideas generation process:

  - Try the technique of word association to develop new channels of thought. Choose three or four verbs, or nouns, at random and then look for the associations between these words. Develop these themes and finally link back to your original goal statement.

  - Select several analogies that capture the essence of your goal. Produce actual solutions to the analogical

---

[2] Portigal, S. (2012) *The Power of Bad Ideas*. Core 77. Available from: www.core77.com/posts/22446/the-power-of-bad-ideas-22446 [24 August 2017].

goal; now translate these back to your actual goal statement.

- Generate some 'get fired' ideas, i.e. ones which would solve, or reduce, the problem, but that are so outlandish that your work colleagues may seriously consider your sanity if you presented them in a business meeting.

- Try posing some questions that open up possibilities, or challenge the way people think. Make sure you include questions about what it will feel like to experience this new thing, or operate in this new way.

- Think about what you don't know about the problem or goal.

- Ask, 'How will we know when we are successful? What will be the visible indicators that we will be able to see?'

- Ask, 'Will others be able to see and value the same indicators of success or does success look different for them? If it looks different, how is it different?'

- Ask yourself, 'If we can fix this issue, what other opportunities might it open up?'

Ideally, as you try some or all of these techniques you should also think about how you can take them into the field and use them alongside the receiving community; how you can quickly move from an idea to a cheap and small experiment. Rapidly prototyping around the ideas gives you additional insight and builds upon the knowledge you are creating.

In an organisational sense, creativity isn't about being a naturally gifted genius or prodigy. It comes from asking good questions, seeing possibilities or opportunities and having the courage to try something new and different. Understand that most of the ideas will go nowhere, but in generating them you will have enriched your understanding and built upon your life experience.

If you want to open yourself up to creativity, you need to open yourself up to new things and new ways of working and being.

Never say never. Always ask why. And never dismiss anything as silly or irrelevant.

Think off the wall, weird, wacky, way out, out of the box; as Arthur C. Clarke put it so succinctly:

> Any sufficiently advanced technology is indistinguishable from magic.[3]

THINGS FOR YOU TO WORK ON NOW

Below are some questions that will help you better understand your own attitude to creativity and how the things you say and do can open up or close down your creative instincts and those of the people around you.

KEY QUESTIONS TO ASK YOURSELF

- When did you last place yourself in an unusual situation?

- How open is your mind? How quick are you to judge the ideas of others, or close down thinking in order to arrive at a decision?

- In collaborative situations, what sort of words do you use and what effect do they have on the dynamic of the group?

- When working in a group, how much of your time do you spend getting your point of view across and heard? Compare this with how much time you spend appreciating the ideas of others and asking questions that help others to contribute ideas.

- What gives you the best feeling – being right, or helping others give voice to new, or radical, ideas?

---

[3] Clarke, A.C. (2000) *Profiles of the Future: an enquiry into the limits of the possible.* London: Indigo.

- How do you feel when people meet your ideas with negative comments about why they won't work, or how they have been tried before?

- How often do you display a 'can do' attitude, rather than a negative (it's going to be difficult, costly, risky, non-standard etc.) attitude? What impact does your response have on the creativity of others?

- When you discover an idea won't work, how quickly do you pick yourself up and start looking for alternatives?

Reflect on your answers to these questions and pick one aspect to work on over the next few weeks. To make this real, you need to think about your approach within the context of a real problem that is both urgent and in need of a new approach.

Below are some suggestions of mini low-risk experiments that will kick-start your creative ability. As you engage in these activities you will be amazed at how you start to see the world differently and how new possibilities open up before your very eyes. You will also find that others start to look at you and value you in a whole new light.

MINI EXERCISES YOU CAN TRY IMMEDIATELY

- Practise brainstorming – for example, list 30 opportunities that 5G and new battery technology could open up for your industry sector and indeed society at large when they arrive.

- The next time you are in a collaborative situation, observe the different behaviours that are produced when someone responds with '**and** ...', rather than '**but** ...'. Which of these words opens up creativity and which of them closes it down? What other words and phrases have the same sort of effect on your group? Monitor what goes on in the group and see if you can change the dynamic of the whole group by the interventions that you make, rather than the ideas that you contribute.

- Place yourself in an unusual situation – for example, if you are a web designer working on a mobile app, knock up a dozen different screen interfaces and then take them into your local coffee shop and get real people to experiment with them. Listen to the feedback and then go back again the next day with another 10 ideas. The important thing is to hear the voice of the consumer as they live the experience of engaging with your products, or services.

- If you are faced with a particularly difficult challenge, go and ask someone who you are absolutely convinced knows nothing about your challenge and could not possibly have anything of value to contribute. Listen carefully to their daft questions and ideas. You may get a real surprise and realise that their questions are not so daft after all.

- Think of one of the new big up-and-coming technological advances, for example blockchain or robotics, and think of at least 10 ways your organisation could use and benefit from it.

If you are inspired to find out more about any of the themes covered in this chapter we suggest that you start by reviewing the resources listed below.

FURTHER FOOD FOR THE CURIOUS

- Goleman, D. (1995) *Emotional Intelligence*. New York: Bantam Books

  - A very comprehensive text on the subject of emotional intelligence.

- Hayashi, A. (2001) 'When to trust your gut'. *Harvard Business Review*, 79 (2). 59–65.

  - A short, yet excellent, article exploring and helping to explain the mechanics of 'gut' instinct.

- Kelly, T. and Kelly, D. (2012) 'Reclaim your creative confidence'. *Harvard Business Review*, 90 (12). 115–118.

  - Excellent and thought-provoking short article that outlines the four steps that underpin the work of the world-renowned design company IDEO and Stanford University School. A must-read for all leaders committed to increasing creativity and innovation.

- Leonard, D. and Straus, S. (1997) 'Putting your company's whole brain to work'. *Harvard Business Review*, 75 (4). 110–121.

  - A well-constructed article focusing on the business imperative to innovate and how to harness the different thinking styles in a process of 'creative abrasion'.

3 DEVELOPING YOURSELF THROUGH MENTORING AND COACHING OTHERS

The focus of this chapter is on how to become more purposeful about your informal sources of learning. It is about starting to see every interaction with other people as an opportunity for your own learning.

Increasingly you will be expected as a leader to take a primary role in mentoring and coaching members of your team. In this chapter we will not specifically address **how** you go about mentoring or coaching as most organisations have a preferred model, but we will direct your attention towards certain core practices that are common to all. Our focus here is primarily upon what you can gain from the process of mentoring and coaching others and how you can become more sensitive to your own developmental needs, drivers and interests so that you can learn and grow even more as a leader.

WHY IS THIS IMPORTANT?

If you really want to understand and know something, teaching it to someone else is the fastest and most effective way. The act of trying to help others to understand causes you to look at an issue in more depth and to reduce it to simple component parts. As you try to put yourself in the learner's place, you will be forced to answer questions that you had not thought of before and you will start to look at problems from completely different angles.

This is not a new idea.

> To teach is to learn twice.
>
> Joseph Joubert (1754–1824)

Seeing things through the eyes of other people and grappling anew with ideas that you had stopped questioning are sure-fire ways of kick-starting your own learning process.

The message is clear: you learn most when you help others to learn or see anew. This is because to help others learn or see things differently, you have to view things from their perspective, understand how they think and re-examine things that you may not have questioned for years.

Mentoring and coaching are not about telling; they are about asking and questioning.

As a team leader you have probably become very good at briefing your team on what needs to be done. You think through what needs to be achieved, work out what steps need to be completed, choose who is best suited to the task and then thoroughly brief them on what they have to do and the standards you expect. All of this is good, but it is not the same as mentoring or coaching.

When you mentor, your aim is to improve knowledge or experience by providing guidance, affirmation or reassurance to your mentee.

When you coach, your aim is release the latent potential in your coachee by asking really good and searching questions that kick-start their learning process. Mentoring and coaching are about guiding and helping people to learn rather than telling them what to do.

So, a key tool of mentoring and coaching is the art of asking powerful questions. The most powerful questions are those that cause others to surface the deeply held, and often unconscious, assumptions that dictate how they see and interpret situations. It is these interpretations that govern people's natural choices and actions and stop them thinking differently.

As you become practised at asking powerful questions you will be amazed at how people suddenly see possibilities that they were previously oblivious to. The act of helping others to see differently will inevitably have a profound effect on the way you see things yourself.

The development of the people in your team is a fundamental role of management. But it is more than just altruism; it is your own route to self-development.

Evidence from Google's Project Oxygen, a long-term internal study to improve the quality of their own management, indicates that being a good coach is the greatest differentiating factor between good and great managers and is far more important than technical ability.[1]

Do not think of mentoring and coaching as something you do in addition to your day job, or as something that requires different skills that you don't have time to perfect. Being a good mentor and a coach is far more important than technical proficiency when it comes to growing your team and yourself as a leader. The skills you develop as a mentor and a coach are the skills that will mark you out as a leader who others want to follow, one capable of making a real difference.

THE IMPACT OF THE ISSUE

Far too many people within organisations believe that, in order to succeed, everyone else must fail. Sadly, this mental model

---

[1] Grote, D. (2016) 'Every manager needs to practice two types of coaching'. *Harvard Business Review*. Available from: https://hbr.org/2016/09/every-manager-needs-to-practice-two-types-of-coaching [22 November 2017].

is reinforced by endless reality TV shows that depict hapless people being evicted, or fired, whilst the alpha male (or female) tramples over the broken bodies in their quest for personal glory.

Don't get us wrong; we have no problem with competition or with the idea of winners. Nor is this about being nice or meek; this is about helping others and, by doing so, helping yourself.

> When you take the time to develop others, you are making a big investment in developing yourself. This is a win–win situation.

When you expand your own potential and that of the people around you, great things can happen and it will show in the way that you and your team perform. Let's look at the story of Tony, a self-employed front-end web developer.

> Tony typically took on challenging short-term contracts and had built an enviable track record delivering leading-edge solutions for a range of blue chip companies around Europe. He was hired to lead a team of 15 developers on a business-critical project that was already in trouble. Tony was performance driven and believed that team building and skills transfer were as much key strengths as his technical ability. He was confident that he could quickly knock his team into shape and get the project back on track.
>
> Three months into the project Tony felt that he had made good progress. The project was back on schedule, he had instituted new practices and most importantly the client appeared to be really happy with the functionality of early release beta modules. He was looking forward to his first contract review meeting and expected praise and a big bonus. Imagine his surprise when the IT director gave him the following feedback:

Tony, the project is on track and we are really impressed by your drive and technical excellence but you have achieved this by focusing all your efforts on your four best developers and driving them into the ground. The result is that these four are on their knees and at least one of them is actively looking for another job; meanwhile, the rest of the team are demoralised, they feel you don't listen to them, don't trust them and only give them routine tasks with no level of challenge. The overall impact is that we cannot see any skills transfer taking place and, although the project is in better shape, the team is now in a worse place than when we hired you.

Tony could not recognise himself in this description. He had no idea any of his team felt like this; he had felt good about himself and assumed that because what he was doing was producing good results, management would be pleased. There was some good news: at the end of the interview the IT director offered to give Tony a two-week sabbatical to attend a coaching skills course at the company's US headquarters. If the feedback from the course was good, Tony would be allowed to continue leading the team with a further review in three months' time. Before ending the interview they agreed personal targets for Tony to achieve on the coaching programme and developmental targets for every member of the team during the first eight weeks after the course.

The course was an eye-opener for Tony. He realised that his high level of technical ability and personal confidence meant that his normal mode of operation was to directly impose his will on others. He was not good at listening to people because that took time and he needed action. He didn't ask questions; he issued instructions. The two big things he picked up from the course were how to really listen without jumping to judgements and how to ask questions that helped his team to think for themselves.

Tony returned to the team with a new attitude and approach. It was hard work for him and he had lots of lapses along the way, but he made a personal commitment to really make coaching work for himself and his team. The next review went really well and brought with it the longed-for praise and bonus.

Tony continued to work on his coaching skills, his contract was extended and in his new role he was asked to roll out a coaching culture to the broader development team.

Tony's story illustrates two really important points. The first is that Tony had very little self-awareness: he was so driven and confident of his own approach that he failed to pick up on the feedback that his team could give him. He didn't see any inadequacies in his style so he did not feel any need to learn or try a different approach. The second important lesson is that Tony had always achieved success by playing to his strengths, yet the feedback from the IT Director took him into a new scary place where he had no experience, no natural aptitude and where he was very vulnerable.

To Tony's credit, he rose to the challenge and over time learned to really value and exploit the new range of interpersonal skills that lie at the heart of the coaching method. As a result, Tony developed as a manager and leader and the nature of the assignments he accepted subtly changed. Now, three years on, he is more valued for his ability to inspire teams and develop people than he is for his ability to develop great websites.

MAKING SENSE OF IT ALL

Many organisations have formalised coaching as a core component of the leader's role. Whatever coaching model your organisation employs, you will need to perfect four key skill sets. These can easily be remembered by the acronym RACE: **r**elationship building, **a**ctive listening, **c**onstructive feedback, **e**ffective questioning.

These four skills are equally relevant when mentoring; however, as a mentor, you also need to be more experienced and knowledgeable as to the task in hand.

- **Relationship building** – if you want to get someone to open up and to be prepared to work with you, you'll need to develop trust-based relationships and be able to establish a good rapport.

- **Active listening** – when you listen properly to someone you will increase their ability to express themselves. When you actively listen to someone you need to put them centre stage and let go of your own thoughts and self-importance.

- **Constructive feedback** – regular, open and transparent feedback is critical for learning and growth. Feedback needs to be constructive, motivating and balanced. In the context of coaching and mentoring you will always need to keep in the back of your mind the thought that the development of others is your prime objective.

- **Effective questioning** – this is the essence of coaching; by asking the right type of questions you tap into your coachees' or mentees' thought processes and take them on a voyage of self-discovery. You will be empowering them to think and act with new confidence and conviction.

It is no coincidence that these four key skills are not only the cornerstone of being an effective coach but also fundamental to developing yourself as a leader.

As you develop as a coach or mentor you will also develop as a leader. The key to attaining your full potential is learning.

Learning is not a solitary process that is only conducted when you are on a course or with your head in a book. Coaching and mentoring are not about telling people what to do; they are a collaborative process of mutual discovery. As you guide and help others to develop you will learn and develop yourself.

PRACTICAL ADVICE

Your first step in shaping your own learning approach is to develop the skills an effective coach needs. The following advice is structured around the four steps of the RACE model.

Relationship building

Working relationships are based on trust, so when we talk about building a relationship we are first and foremost asking how you gain the trust of others. It is worth remembering President John F. Kennedy's words in his 1961 inaugural address:

> Ask not what your country can do for you but what you can do for your country.[2]

You build trust by focusing first on the needs of others. Don't enter a conversation with a list of your own needs but rather ask questions to surface what your listener needs and what you may be able to do to help.

Take an interest in the person you are coaching or mentoring. For most people, their favourite topic is either themselves or the achievements of members of their family. Listen carefully; this is how you get to know someone and find out about their values and what is important to them.

Develop the ability to converse on a wide range of subjects and look for areas of common interest: maybe you have kids at the same stage of schooling, or you both love a particular cuisine or support the same football team. Making a safe connection

---

[2] Read the entire speech here: www.jfklibrary.org/Research/Research-Aids/Ready-Reference/JFK-Quotations/Inaugural-Address.aspx [13 November 2017].

at a human level will help you to make a connection at a professional level.

Demonstrate empathy and sensitivity to moods and feelings. Accept that everyone has a valid point of view even if you do not agree with it. If you can learn how they see the world, and why they see it like they do, you'll be better placed to understand their behaviour and the decisions they make, and assess how you can help them. You never know – you may even change your view!

Demonstrate modesty and humility and be prepared to admit your mistakes or that you are wrong. Develop your sense of humour and your ability to laugh at yourself.

> Remember, you can't force someone to be coached or mentored so it must be elective and built upon a foundation of trust.

Active listening

Active listening is easier said than done. It requires concentration, mindfulness, authenticity, openness, receptivity and intuition. When you focus on someone else with the intention of really listening to them, the sense of yourself will diminish and you will start to see the world through their eyes. This is empathy in action.

> What stops you from listening in any situation is yourself: either you get distracted by your own thoughts or ideas, or you simply don't make the effort to focus on the other person.

Therefore, resist any temptation to give your own examples of a similar situation to someone else, as this turns the attention away from them and back to you.

Listening happens at different levels. Most of the time, most people do what might be termed 'internal listening'. You take a position of listening, you may even look the speaker in the eye and nod occasionally, but actually most of your focus is internal – on your own concerns and feelings. Often you listen just long enough to find an opportunity to interrupt and give your own opinion. Or you may be focusing on the phraseology of your next question or point you wish to make. Your focus of attention is yourself!

What you are aiming for is '360-degree listening'. Here you are not only fully focused on what the other person is saying, you are also tuned in to how they are saying it and sensing their emotional connection to the ideas, what excites them and why.

Here are some key tips to improve the quality of your listening:

- When a team member asks you what to do about a situation, resist the temptation to give an answer off the cuff. Start by asking what they think and what ideas they have. Then follow up with a question as to the likely consequences of their suggestions.

- Go and talk to people – without an agenda. Get them talking about a favourite subject or passion in life. Listen, learn and embrace the silences.

- Don't pass judgement on anything that you are told and don't try to impose your values. Ask questions to help you understand where the speaker is coming from and why they believe what they do.

- If your attention wanders, paraphrase back or take a few notes to help redirect your attention back to the other person.

Constructive feedback

Providing developmental feedback is a key managerial skill. Feedback can and should be provided to your peers and your bosses. The tone may be subtly different depending on whether it is given upwards, downwards or sideways. The basic principles, however, remain the same every time.

In most working environments, feedback is sadly lacking; feedback is both a learning and a motivational tool. Many managers are reluctant to give negative feedback; however, recent research suggests that they are even more reluctant about providing positive feedback in the form of praise.[3] The research suggests that many managers correlate their personal assessment of their own effectiveness with how they give negative feedback, but the recipients base their assessment of their manager on how they deliver positive feedback. Genuine, honest and, when appropriate, public praise is very important: it motivates, boosts morale and builds confidence, team relationships and trust. Learning to get better at delivering feedback is a win–win for everyone.

When giving feedback, focus on both the positives and the negatives – everyone needs to feel valued and appreciated. In addition, if people are to progress they also need to understand their areas for improvement.

Here are some general rules for giving feedback:

- Helpful feedback:
  - is easy to understand and put into context;
  - is specific and direct – gives examples and consequences;
  - addresses issues that matter, that are important enough to be commented upon;
  - focuses on behaviour that can be changed;
  - leaves choices for the recipient – uses expressions like 'could do' rather than 'should do';
  - is delivered with openness, honesty and kindness;

---

[3] Zenger, J. and Folkman, J. (2017) 'Why do so many managers avoid giving praise?' *Harvard Business Review*. Available from: https://hbr.org/2017/05/why-do-so-many-managers-avoid-giving-praise [29 November 2017].

- is controlled and objective; don't give feedback when you are under stress or extreme pressure;

- is owned by you – what you believe and what you feel; you are not delivering a third party's message.

- Unhelpful feedback:

- is coded or out of context;

- is general or vague;

- is unimportant or trivial in terms of what needs to be achieved by the team;

- imposes your own values – don't use expressions such as 'that was really stupid';

- makes judgements about attitudes, impact and intentions and decides for someone what they need to change – encourage others to examine, accept and own their own issues;

- is based on hearsay – if you have not witnessed the behaviour for yourself you are not in a position to comment;

- is too prescriptive – focus on required outcomes rather than the process by which they are achieved; leave room for personal choice and, hence, growth;

- compares performance with that of another team member;

- results in hurt feelings, emotional barriers and defensive behaviours.

Feedback should be a continual process; it should be regular and timely. Always consider the likely impact of your feedback on the receiver before leaping in.

Always remember: you can criticise someone's behaviour and the resulting consequences but you should never criticise them as a person.

Effective questioning

Effective questions are easy to understand; they are worded so that the person answering only needs to work on forming their response rather than trying to understand the question. Effective questions also have a clear sense of purpose; for example, to gather more information, see something from another perspective, or create a sense of the future.

Think carefully about the purpose of your questions as a coach or mentor. What sort of thinking are you trying to elicit in your coachee or mentee? You will find examples of six different types of coaching and mentoring questions below. Some of the time you may be working with people who have little experience or confidence in their own ability. At other times you may be working with someone who is overconfident or thinks that they are always right and does not listen to the views of others. As you ask questions, you are trying to get them to become more aware of their situation, to read the signs in front of them and to start to build up a mental image of how and why things work the way they do. So, the first pair of questions tend to be focused on past events and aimed at gathering more information or explaining, describing and clarifying events:

- **Probing questions** – these invite more detail, and can be used to open up thinking or clarify a situation. They may take the following forms:

  - Can you tell me more about ...?

  - What was the first thing you noticed when ...?

  - What were you trying to do when you first noticed this issue?

  - Who else may be able to throw light on this one?

  - Have we had any other issues reported that are similar?

- **Analytical questions** – these seek to explore cause and effect. They may take the following forms:

- What sequence of events preceded ...?

- What did you think would happen if you structured your data search in this way?

- What is the next thing the customer service adviser does after they have confirmed the client identity?

- What might happen if we integrate 'x' with 'y'?

Notice that analytical questions are often posed in the past tense – they are seeking to rationalise past events – but analytical questions can be projected into the future to speculate how things might turn out. The final bullet point shows how you might structure a future-focused question.

As you start out as a coach, mentor or, indeed, as a manager, you will find that the vast majority of your questions are probing or analytical in nature. But as you move on and become more practised and adept at active listening you will start to move away from a focus on events and start to examine how people think and feel and how what they think and feel shapes how they perform. The next pair of questions are used to explore context and the social and emotional structures within which we operate.

- **Reflective questions** – these questions are introspective and individual. They challenge people to think about why they hold the views they do and to examine their own motivations. They may take the following forms:

  - Why do you believe that ...?

  - What are your key concerns about ...?

  - What would need to change for you to feel comfortable about ...?

You should see immediately that these sorts of questions are the ones that, as a good leader, you should be asking yourself all the time in order to build your own self-awareness.

- **Affective questions** – these are used to bring to light information about how people feel on a topic, exploring the emotional aspects of a situation. They may take the following forms:

- Why was there such resistance to our changes to the ...?

- How is the change in 'x' impacting morale?

- What would it feel like to work in an organisation that ...?

In our experience, most leaders are very poor at these sorts of questions. In our story of Tony earlier in the chapter we see an example of a leader who had very poor self-awareness but also no appreciation of how his style was impacting his team. If he had engaged in affective questioning he would have gained a more rounded understanding of his situation. You can see from the examples listed that these questions can be positioned to reflect past, current or future thinking.

The final two types of questions are used to challenge conventional wisdom and to generate new ideas. If phrased well they can act as a powerful catalyst for change. These are among the most impactful questions a coach or mentor can ask and are usually posed in the future tense.

- **Explorative questions** – these open up new avenues of enquiry and look for potential synergy. They may take the following forms:

  - What new things would you be able to achieve if ...?

  - Who else could benefit from ...?

  - What else could you do that would make this even more ...?

- **Fresh questions** – these challenge 'eternal truths' and basic thinking. They are used for assumption busting. They can lead to breakthrough ideas and innovation. They may take the following forms:

  - Why can't you just ...?

  - From our customers' point of view, what is the 'job to be done'?

- If you could start with a blank sheet of paper, how would you ...?

You will note that all the questions above are open in their intent and not leading, or restricted by an anticipated answer. Using questions like this is not an easy skill and needs practice. But remember that questions trigger both thinking and action so you need to ask the right questions to trigger the sort of thinking that you are aiming for, and this will increase the likelihood of different actions and outcomes. Your role as coach or mentor is to help your coachee or mentee shape their thoughts, reflections and ideas into an appropriate way forward that helps them grow both as a professional and in the rounder sense of being human.

The ideas we have suggested above are not meant to be prescriptive; they are about getting better at the four elements of the RACE model and, as a consequence, learning through developing others and becoming a better leader. We suggest that you look at them and use them as inspiration to craft your own set of actions to try out.

The primary focus of your activity is to open the door to new experiences, relationships and challenges and, in so doing, drive new ways of thinking and feeling that produce opportunities for personal learning and growth.

THINGS FOR YOU TO WORK ON NOW

Below are some questions that will help you to become more conscious of your own learning as you coach or mentor members of your team. Use your new understanding to shape how you interact with your team when you are coaching and mentoring them. Don't forget to build in time for personal reflection and learning. As a result, you will become a better leader and your team will become a happier and more productive unit.

KEY QUESTIONS TO ASK YOURSELF

- What can I do to raise my own awareness of how my actions are perceived and how they shape the way others judge me?

- How good am I at using questions that challenge my team members to think and feel differently about situations? What can I do to be better?

- What can I do to help my team to better understand themselves so that they can perform better?

- How much time and effort do I spend helping others to learn new ways of thinking and looking at problems?

- What have I learned in the last week as a direct result of helping others to learn?

- What emphasis did I place on my own learning during my last appraisal cycle?

Reflect on your answers to the above questions and pick one aspect to work on over the next few weeks.

Below are some suggestions about things you can work on that will help you to better understand your own progress at perfecting the four core skills of coaching and mentoring.

MINI EXERCISES YOU CAN TRY IMMEDIATELY

- Talk through a pressing issue with a colleague you trust and respect. Ask them if you can record the conversation. That night, review the conversation and focus particularly on the questions you asked and the way those questions steered the conversation or opened up new avenues. Use the guide on pages 51 to 54 to review your use of questioning.

- Use the analysis above to identify one area of questioning that you want to work on. In all your coaching, mentoring or feedback meetings with your team consciously plan how you can use this questioning technique.

- Keep a log of how often you give direct feedback to your team over the course of a week. Check that you are giving fair, appropriate and deserved positive and developmental feedback to each member of your team. If this is not the case, make an action plan to rebalance the frequency and nature of the feedback you give.

If you are inspired to find out more about any of the themes covered in this chapter we suggest that you start by reviewing the resources listed below.

FURTHER FOOD FOR THE CURIOUS

- Andersen, E. (2016) 'Managing yourself learning to learn: mental tools to help you master new skills'. *Harvard Business Review*, March. 98–101.

  - Concise guide on how to grow your powers of self-awareness and curiosity whilst dealing with the feelings of vulnerability that come with taking on new ways of thinking and acting.

- Grote, D. (2016) 'Every manager needs to practice two types of coaching'. *Harvard Business Review*. Available from: https://hbr.org/2016/09/every-manager-needs-to-practice-two-types-of-coaching [22 November 2017].

  - An excellent short and very readable paper that stresses the importance of dialogue-based coaching, both at regular agreed intervals and in response to events that trigger learning opportunities.

- Zenger, J. and Folkman, J. (2017) 'Why do so many managers avoid giving praise'. *Harvard Business Review*. Available from: https://hbr.org/2017/05/why-do-so-many-managers-avoid-giving-praise [29 November 2017].

  - This well-researched article gives some surprising statistics about giving both critical feedback and praise. It suggests that, on average, managers overestimate the value of giving negative feedback and greatly underestimate the value that can be accrued from positive feedback.

4 PLAYING THE POLITICAL GAME WHILST MAINTAINING INTEGRITY

The focus of this chapter is on differences of opinion. Where the future is concerned there are no right or wrong answers. What there are, are choices; only hindsight will prove any choice to be a good one or a poor one. The advice in this chapter will help you to join in the key conversations that always accompany controversial change and decision making within your organisation; it will do so in a way that ensures your voice is heard and you are not marginalised.

WHY IS THIS IMPORTANT?

In the workplace, organisational politics are a fact of life. Organisations, being made up of people, are essentially political institutions. All business professionals need to be adept at dealing with political situations, but some are better at it than others.

Unfortunately, there is, however, no single formula for success. Politics are often messy, ambiguous and unpredictable; and to top it all, being right is not enough. Outcomes in the political arena depend upon the subtle interactions and interplays between people. Each situation will be different and unique, and what proves successful in one situation may prove disastrous in the next. In essence, organisational politics are an art, rather than a science!

Political acumen is a key skill for anyone wanting to 'get things done', to have influence over others, to invoke change, to make an impact and to build and maintain their reputation.

THE IMPACT OF THE ISSUE

Organisational politics are often construed as being destructive, time wasting or unethical. Ask anyone what words and phrases spring to mind when you mention the words 'organisational politics' and, 9 times out of 10, you will get responses such as:

- doing deals;
- scoring points;
- personal agendas;
- getting one over on one's colleagues;
- secrecy and subterfuge;
- mafioso tactics;
- win–lose situations.

Organisational politics are, however, simply the result of differing opinions, values, standpoints, perceptions and so on. As such, they can be dealt with either positively or negatively. On the positive side, organisational politics are about:

- influence;
- collaboration;
- building relationships;
- openness and honesty;
- being streetwise;
- win–win situations.

Participating in organisational politics is not an option, but how you choose to participate is. The choice is yours, either positively or negatively, and the outcomes are of your own making.

MAKING SENSE OF IT ALL

Researchers Baddeley and James studied leaders who had attained long-term political success within their organisation.[1] The leaders attributed their success to the following two key dimensions:

- acting from an informed and knowledgeable position that demonstrates:
  - an understanding of the decision-making processes of your organisation;
  - an awareness of the overt and covert agendas of the key decision makers;
  - an innate understanding of who has the power and what gives them that power;
  - a willingness to go that extra mile to help others even if it is not part of your job description;
  - an understanding of the style and culture of your organisation;
  - a sense of the meaning of 'politics' in the context of your organisation;
- acting with integrity as defined by the following principles:
  - avoiding playing psychological games with people;
  - accepting yourself and others as human beings who all have their associated strengths, weaknesses, peculiarities, quirks and imperfections;
  - seeking to find win–win strategies in situations of difficulty or conflict.

The model in Figure 4.1 utilises these two dimensions and is adapted from the work of Baddeley and James. Each quadrant of the model is illustrated with an animal analogy to create a political zoo. The **innocent sheep** acts with integrity, but has

---

[1] Baddeley, S. and James, K. (1987) 'Owl, fox, donkey, sheep: political skills for managers'. *Management Education and Development*, 18 (1). 3–19.

no clue about what is going on in the organisational sense. The **clever fox** knows precisely what is going on, but uses this knowledge to exploit the weaknesses of others. The **inept baboon** neither acts with integrity nor knows what is going on. The **wise dolphin** possesses both understanding and integrity and hence represents our icon of political success. The behaviour of the four animals is described below in greater detail.

Figure 4.1 Political zoo[2]

Psychological game playing   Acting with integrity

Politically aware

Politically unaware

The **sheep** sees the world through simplistic eyes. Sheep believe you are right if you are in a position of authority. They do what they are told, stick to the rules, are too busy to network and don't know how to build coalitions and alliances. They act with integrity, but are street-naïve.

---

[2] The political zoo is an adaptation of the model developed by Simon Baddeley and Kim James (1987) in 'Owl, fox, donkey, sheep: political skills for managers'. *Management Education and Development*, 18 (1). 3–19.

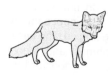

The **fox** knows exactly what is going on, but uses this knowledge to exploit the weaknesses in others. Foxes are self-centred but with a charming veneer. They are manipulative and like games involving winners and losers, and love leading lambs to the slaughterhouse.

The **baboon** is not tuned into the grapevine. Baboons' reception of outside signals is blocked and they therefore end up conspiring with the powerless. They are emotionally illiterate, seeing things in black and white and not recognising when they are fighting a losing battle. They play games with people, but don't understand why they keep losing.

The **dolphin** takes account of other people personally. Dolphins are excellent listeners and aware of others' viewpoints. They are non-defensive, open, and share information. They use creativity and imagination to engineer win–win situations. They act from both an informed and an ethical standpoint; they are both streetwise and virtuous.

What characterises dolphins is calmness in a storm, a certainty about their own destiny and a thirst to learn from others. They may be busy, but not stressed or pressured; and they can always find the time to work alongside colleagues or help others out. People have respect for them as model human beings first, and for their competence in their professional capacity second.

PRACTICAL ADVICE

You will inevitably behave as each of the four animals from time to time; however, it is your default position or your prime behaviour that counts. The aim of this book is to help you move to the top of the model; left or right is, however, your choice. We sincerely hope, though, that your aim would be to become a 'dolphin'. Here are a few examples of how the four animals would behave in various situations:

- **When in situations of conflict**
  - The **dolphin** asks, 'How can we work together to solve this one?'
  - The **fox** asserts, 'I am not prepared to change my position.'
  - The **baboon** declares, 'I can't agree and would prefer not to discuss it anyway.'
  - The **sheep** mutters, 'I concede the point and will accept whatever you say.'

- **When responding to or giving orders**
  - The **dolphin** looks for opportunities to go beyond the call of duty, to extend their sphere of influence and to develop the potential in others.
  - The **fox** demands, 'Do as you are told – it's my way or the highway.'
  - The **baboon** protests, 'That's outside my brief – I won't do it.'
  - The **sheep** says meekly, 'I will do as you say.'

- **When communicating with others**
  - The **dolphin** actively listens, is open and shares information.
  - The **fox** is dismissive of alternative viewpoints, looks for a fight and believes that information is power.
  - The **baboon** whinges and moans to others who are equally powerless.
  - The **sheep** keeps its head down and keeps quiet about anything potentially controversial.

- **When considering the phrase 'organisational politics'**

  - The **dolphin** believes that organisational politics are a fact of life and are about influence, collaboration and achieving win–win outcomes.

  - The **fox** believes that organisational politics are a sport. They are about winners and losers and about coming out on top; they involve manipulation and exploitation to achieve one's own ends.

  - The **baboon** believes that organisational politics are a game, but doesn't understand why it keeps losing.

  - The **sheep** believes that it does not enter into the game of organisational politics – it is just everyone else!

Consider your own behaviour: which of the political animals best represents your behaviour today within your current role and which do you aspire to become? If 'dolphinism' is your aim, the five single most important things you can do are as follows:

- **Develop your network** – build positive relationships with anyone and everyone; create allies and advocates, build coalitions and alliances. Use your network to find out what is going on, to learn, to acquire those nuggets of wisdom and to tap into the organisational grapevine.

- **Be someone that can be trusted** – always do what you say you will do; never give people false hopes. Do not give empty promises because it is the easiest thing to do, and genuinely mean what you say. Remember, when it comes to trust, actions speak louder than words.

- **Be generous** – give a little of yourself to others, whether that is your time, your expertise, your knowledge, your help or your support, without expecting anything in return. Look for the positive in others, assume they have good intentions and stay curious to find out what these are even when they are not obvious or the person is behaving negatively. Be prepared to forgive and offer people a face-saving route if they need to change their minds or behave differently.

- **Listen and learn** – actively listen to others, focus on what they are saying rather than thinking about what you are going to say next. Accept what they say without judgement or criticism, try to put yourself in their shoes and view the situation from their perspective – you may learn something that surprises you. Remember that perception is reality in the eye of the beholder.

- **Look for the win–win** – if you want somebody to do something for you, always consider why they should do it: the 'What's in it for them?' question. Think about why you do things that others have asked of you, or why you haven't, as the case may be. It may be because you like the person, because it is an interesting task or because it will enhance your skills or reputation. It could be to gain 'brownie' points, because you owe someone, or to build trust or of course for many, many more reasons. People are far more likely to do something that you want them to do if there is something in it for them. Learn people's motivators and tap into them; this way you will engage both hearts and minds.

Tom, an interim manager, had been brought in to help with the merging of two IT functions with dissimilar remuneration and benefit packages. Tom took the mantle of handling all the negotiations with representatives from both IT functions and also senior management. Through his openness and honesty, he struck an 'affordable' deal whereby everyone would receive some of the basic benefits straight away, for example free lunches, whilst remuneration packages would be slowly adjusted over a five-year period. He subsequently won the trust and support of everyone concerned. The departmental representatives ended up being the ones who outlined the deal and the process to their own colleagues.

Of all the animals, the fox is the one that is instantly recognisable and by far the most difficult to deal with, hence we will now focus on foxes.

Dealing with the foxes of the world

Foxes are self-centred, and senior ones are also invariably egotistical too whilst the more junior ones may be narcissistic. Your tactics for handling such individuals may include:

- Make them feel good about themselves:
    - Help them to develop their skills and to shine at something.
    - Build on their suggestions – use the words 'yes **and** ...' to steer them, rather than 'yes, **but** ...'.
    - Help them to think through the consequences of their actions by using coaching-style questioning techniques.
    - Offer them the 'limelight'.
    - Massage their ego and praise their intellect.
    - Get them to talk about themselves – remember this is most people's favourite subject. This will also have the added benefit of allowing you to get to know your 'enemy'.
- Make them feel comfortable about you:
    - Help them to understand you – your values and drivers.
    - Be truthful and transparent.
- Don't give them any ammunition:
    - Be firm and strong.
    - Don't be sloppy or slapdash.
    - Keep your cool.

- Protect yourself:
  - Cultivate your friends – there is safety in numbers.
  - Cultivate allies – this will limit the fox's sphere of influence.
  - Keep positive about yourself and maintain your values.

Remember, always consider why anyone should do something for you: what's in it for them?

The following mini case illustrates how a relatively junior IT manager successfully dealt with a fox and prevented a flawed change initiative from having a detrimental impact on his organisation.

A medium-sized financial services company had just implemented a new Customer Relationship Management (CRM) system; however, it had not delivered the anticipated business benefit. Indeed, in some quarters it had started to receive considerable criticism; most notably from the Banking Director, who claimed that productivity in his department had gone down since the implementation of the new system. The reason for this is that the new CRM system, being so much richer in (unused) functionality, takes 10 screens of form filling compared to the old system which used two. In addition, the new CRM system screens contain a significant number of redundant fields. So laborious is the form-filling process that staff are now writing details onto pieces of paper as they talk to customers, for fear that customers will get tired of waiting; they then enter the data after the customer has been dealt with. This is clearly not welcome to the Banking Director.

The new CRM system had cost some £20 million to implement and the Chief Information Officer (CIO) was keen to demonstrate a return on his investment. The CIO was considering his options, which were:

- To do nothing; the system was working and supporting the business need – why not put it down to experience?

- To spread the use of the system into the growing European operation – £20 million spread over the UK and the six continental European countries would soften the impact of the costs considerably.

- To spend more money and sort out the user interface issues – rationalising the number of screens and removing the redundant fields.

- To try to pass some of the blame onto the business for failing to adapt their processes to fit in with the new system.

The CIO in this case was a foxy character with an eye on promotion. His first reaction was to take option 4 but this was soon discounted as unrealistic. Therefore, option 2 became the CIO's favoured route forward.

However, a relatively junior IT manager involved in the project challenged the CIO's rationale. He followed the CIO to the coffee machine one day and started asking questions about the project; general ones to start – 'What are your views on the new CRM system?' – and then more specific questions, such as: 'How do you believe we can improve our return on investment?'; 'How much resistance do you perceive from the Europeans?' (who didn't want the new CRM and who could become powerful antagonists); and, 'Could there be a better way of achieving value from the CRM?'

By asking such questions he helped the CIO to think through the consequences of his actions: that the CRM system was a solution looking for a problem, and that trying to force the Europeans to have something they didn't want could backfire terribly and make the problem even worse. These factors would ultimately have a negative impact on the CIO's own reputation.

Again through questioning, the junior manager then helped the CIO to come up with an alternative solution that was both a win for the company and a win for the CIO. They redeveloped the front end of the CRM system and packaged it up for sale elsewhere within the group – the Hong Kong office got something it desperately needed, the European operation was not forced to have something it did not want and the UK IT department became a profit centre. All these factors enhanced the reputation of the CIO.

Baboons can be dealt with in a similar way to foxes but they will be easier to negotiate with or neutralise – they have a tendency to 'dig their own graves'.

Sheep are well meaning so can become targets for exploitation; you may therefore need to boost their self-confidence and protect them from the foxes of the world.

THINGS FOR YOU TO WORK ON NOW

Below are some questions that will help you build a picture of how tuned in you are to the way in which you behave and how your actions may be perceived and interpreted by your work colleagues.

KEY QUESTIONS TO ASK YOURSELF

- Within my current role, which of the political 'animals' do I believe I now behave most like, and which do I aspire to become?

- Do I always fulfil my promises; do my deeds always match my words?

- How extensive is my network and how much effort do I dedicate towards extending it?

- How aware am I of what goes on in the broader organisational context?

- How attuned am I to my organisation's grapevine – am I the first or the last to find out what is afoot?

- How attuned am I to the personal agendas of my key stakeholders? Do I understand why they make the decisions that they do?

- Do I actively listen to others without judging?

- Do I openly share information?

- Do I do things for others without expecting anything in return?

Reflect on your answers to these questions and pick one aspect to work on over the next few weeks. To make this real, you need to think about your approach within the context of a real organisational situation within which there are winners and losers and actions are contested.

Below are some suggestions about things you can work on that will help you to better understand where you currently sit in the political zoo and how you can transition towards a set of political behaviours that help you influence situations in a positive way.

MINI EXERCISES YOU CAN TRY IMMEDIATELY

- Next time you are just about to agree to do something, reflect for a moment. Do you really intend to do it, are you totally committed, would you move heaven and earth to deliver? If you cannot answer yes to these questions, think again before you commit. Always doing what you say is habit-forming, too.

- Next time you ask someone to do something for you, think about what's in it for them: why would they commit to doing it? Think about what you could offer them or how you could make it more appealing.

- Next time you wish to challenge someone's thinking replace the word '**but**' with an '**and**'.

- When a colleague makes a decision that you do not agree with, try to figure out their motives or rationale – ask them why they made the decision and what they are hoping to achieve. Try to get to the crux of the matter. You may well change your own view or help them to change theirs.

If you are inspired to find out more about any of the themes covered in this chapter we suggest that you start by reviewing the resources listed below.

FURTHER FOOD FOR THE CURIOUS

- Baddeley, S. and James, K. (1987) 'Owl, fox, donkey, sheep: political skills for managers'. *Management Education and Development*, 18 (1). 3–19.

  - A short, but truly inspirational, paper. The ideas presented are just as relevant today as they were at the time of publication.

- Chatham, R. (2015) *The Art of IT Management*. Swindon: BCS.

  - Contains a lot of practical tools and techniques that will help you on your route to 'dolphinism'. It also covers underpinning competencies such as coaching skills and developing your emotional intelligence.

5   MANAGING YOUR OWN TIME

The focus of this chapter is on the decisions you are constantly, and often unconsciously, making about how you invest your time and energy. In an environment where most of us are running faster just to stay in the same place, it is critical that we learn how to balance how we use this most precious of resources – time.

WHY IS THIS IMPORTANT?

Our time is a precious and limited commodity. We buy other people's time to do things we don't want to do, or can't do, and our time is bought by whomever we work for. Most people don't analyse where their time goes – a similar attitude to money is called reckless spending. Here are some thought-provoking quotes on the subject of time:

> How we spend our days is, of course, how we spend our lives.
> Annie Dillard[1]

> If you want something done, ask a busy person.
> Benjamin Franklin

---

[1] Dillard, A. (2013) *The Writing Life*. New York: Harper Perennial.

> Work always expands to fill the time available.
> C. Northcote Parkinson[2]

Most of the technical leaders that we work with never seem to have enough time to do the things they want to do or think they ought to do. Typically, they spend 25 to 35 per cent of their time dealing with their emails. Much of the rest of their time is spent in reactive mode responding to telephone calls, attending meetings, dealing with crises or people that just turn up on their doorstep, and so on – the list is endless.

THE IMPACT OF THE ISSUE

When you are in constant reactive mode you are not being productive. Trying to focus on thoughtful, in-depth tasks can be a challenge these days with the constant lure of incoming emails, the expectation of an instant response, and tasks being fired at us from multiple directions all in an environment of information overload. We live in a frantic world where distractions are constant and, with the rapid pace of technological change, it is only set to get worse. Maura Thomas[3] suggests that traditional time management techniques no longer work – consider the past decade and the dramatic changes in the devices and platforms that we use and the workspaces we occupy.

Traditional time management teaches us to prioritise, but in today's world everything is urgent or a number one priority. Perhaps focus is the key? Think of the many distractions you get each day and the time you may waste agonising over priorities and swapping between activities because you can't decide which is the most important, and searching for things you have lost because you are too busy to organise yourself.

---

[2] Parkinson, C.N. (1955, 19 November) 'Parkinson's Law'. *The Economist*.

[3] Thomas, M. (2015) 'Time management training doesn't work'. *Harvard Business Review*. Available from: https://hbr.org/2015/04/time-management-training-doesnt-work [22 November 2017].

73

Mary, an IT project manager, felt overstretched. She was constantly battling to fit everything in whilst striving to meet unrealistic deadlines. She found herself constantly playing catch-up and started to come to the office earlier and leave later. When this didn't solve the problem, evening and weekend work became the norm. Part of her problem was focus – she had become a 'flutterby', darting from one task to another without finishing anything off and frantically searching for information she had mislaid before going to meetings and hence arriving underprepared. The second part of her problem was delegation. Delegation takes time, time that Mary did not have, so she decided it was quicker to do it herself. Doing it herself led to even more work out of office hours and, of course, you cannot delegate to anyone when you are working from home at the weekend. Mary had got herself into a vicious circle of 'busyness' but she was not being productive.

MAKING SENSE OF IT ALL

Your aim is to be effective in what you do and efficient in the way you do it. However, it is very easy to confuse efficiency with effectiveness; for example, you may scrub floors efficiently, but if this is not what you are paid to do, it is not an effective use of your time.

- Efficiency is time related; it is about doing things the **right way**.
- Effectiveness is goal related; it is about doing the **right things**.

Effectiveness is about doing those things that are important: the tasks, activities and decision making that will help you to achieve your purpose and build the business.

It is relatively straightforward to plan your time based on the urgency of a task; however, it is easy to forget to take into account the importance of a task. Generally speaking, important tasks are the ones that are likely to contribute towards your effectiveness. Importance and urgency are two mutually independent measures; just because a task is urgent, it does not necessarily follow that it is important, or vice versa. Based on these two measures, tasks, therefore, fall into one of four categories, as suggested by Covey in *The 7 Habits of Highly Effective People*.[4]

Tasks that are important but not urgent

These include:

- planning and strategising;
- networking and relationship building;
- developing new opportunities;
- employee training;
- personal development.

Tasks that are urgent but not important

These include:

- interruptions;
- some phone calls and emails;
- many meetings;
- things you hang onto because you like doing them that you should be delegating.

---

[4] US President Eisenhower is quoted as saying, 'What is important is seldom urgent and what is urgent is seldom important.' This idea was brought into management mainstream thinking by Stephen Covey in his business classic *The 7 Habits of Highly Effective People*, first published in the UK by Simon & Schuster in 1989.

Tasks that are neither urgent nor important

These include:

- trivia;
- many phone calls and emails;
- time wasters;
- things you do because you like doing them that do not contribute to your job 'purpose'.

Tasks that are both urgent and important

These include:

- impending deadlines;
- important meetings;
- crisis management;
- fire-fighting;
- emergencies;
- last-minute preparations.

If you do not actively manage your time, it will tend to get swallowed up by activities that fall into the urgent but not important category; this is nearly always at the expense of activities in the important but not urgent category. The consequences of insufficient time on important but not urgent activities such as planning and strategising for the future is rework, fire-fighting and crisis management, which, in turn, leaves even less time for planning and strategising; a vicious circle sets in and you cease to become effective.

In order to get a grip on your time, radical change is often required. This will be needed in two areas – you will need to change what you do yourself and you will need to change what your organisation does to you: the barriers, constraints and demands put upon you. You have control over the former but the latter is more challenging – some of your tactics may be overt by pushing back and some of your tactics may be covert, i.e. by stealth.

In the following story, a CIO pushed back and got his board to support a radical decision in order to get things moving:

A pharmaceutical company was struggling with its IT systems. Due to a series of mergers and acquisitions over the years it had ended up with multiple systems serving similar business needs, numerous legacy systems and a lack of data integrity. As a consequence, it had a very long list of 'things to be changed' with everything being a number one priority. This list served as a massive 'ball and chain' around IT's neck. It served to paralyse activity with many competing commitments and numerous bottlenecks. The CIO made a radical decision – to put all work on hold, bar one major project and a handful of minor ones. The choice criteria was based on the question: 'In a worst-case scenario situation, without this change, would it close the business down and if so for how long?'

The major project that won the day was developing and implementing a disaster recovery procedure. After implementation they picked a second, then a third project. After a time, the test question changed to: 'Will it improve our bottom line and, if so, by how much?'

Two messages are clear in this story; the first is the identification of a clearly understood business priority and the second is an unrelenting focus on that priority.

Focus is key. For every decision and action you take you must ask yourself: 'How does this contribute to the delivery of my key outcome?' If it doesn't contribute to the outcome, why are you doing it?

Our second story is of a young business relationship manager (BRM) who used stealth tactics to neutralise the negative impact of a controlling CIO:

> A highly competitive and controlling CIO played his role as a 'game of warfare' – he decided what the business could and could not have and pitted one department off against another. As a consequence, there was a long list of very minor enhancements to systems that the business could really benefit from that were highly unlikely to ever get implemented. By stealth, the young BRM persuaded the CIO to approve the changes one by one in exchange for favours the business felt happy to agree to. As a consequence, the CIO lost his power and hold over the business and started to see the benefit of a mutually cooperative approach.

Now let's turn to the changes you may wish to make to ensure you spend at least 50 per cent of your time in proactive mode focusing on the future and being productive in your role.

PRACTICAL ADVICE

The challenge for you is to ensure you spend sufficient time on the important but not urgent tasks and minimise the time you spend on the other three types of task identified in the previous section. Go through your calendar for the last three months and see where you spend your time. How do you feel about the balance? Are you spending sufficient time on strategic activities (those that are important but not urgent) as opposed to tactical issues (those that are urgent but not important)? How much of your time is taken up by fire-fighting, an activity that is both urgent and important or wasted on trivial activities that are neither urgent nor important? Now read and act on the following pointers, repeat the calendar exercise in another three months' time and assess your progress.

- **Banish time thieves** – these include junk emails or emails people have copied you into that you don't need to know about, irrelevant meetings, meetings for meetings' sake or people that stop by just for a chat because they are bored:

  - Turn off all email and mobile phone alerts – set email filters to draw your attention to what is important and eliminate the spam. As far as possible, schedule certain times of day to check and deal with your email rather than reacting to each and every alert.

  - Don't have social network sites open on your desktop.

  - Be selective about the meetings you attend – if you do not have a valuable contribution to make, decline the invitation.

  - If someone drops by for a chat, tell them you only have a minute – if they need more, schedule them in at lunchtime or the end of the day. Use non-verbal cues to indicate that their time is up – stand up or put your jacket on.

- **Concentrate** – get to know your own body clock. If you are most productive in the morning, do those tasks that require more brain power then; leave those phone calls that don't require a lot of thought until the afternoon when your energy levels are dwindling:

  - Take mini breaks – a simple five-minute walk to the coffee machine can do wonders to recharge your batteries.

  - Remember to eat – we need fuel to maintain our energy levels and the right type of fuel. Avoid heavy meals that take energy to digest and sugary snacks that cause your blood-sugar levels to yo-yo; instead, go for complex carbohydrates and small amounts of protein that provide you with a slow and sustained release of energy.

  - Do one thing at a time – you can only concentrate effectively on one thing; therefore, only have one task in front of you at any one time and remove any distracting 'clutter'.

79

- **Delegate** – delegate tasks to grow the people who report to you and to create space in your diary for other activities. Effective delegation is not easy. The principal challenges are as follows:

  - The initial overhead when we delegate a task for the first time. It is probably true that, in the short term, we could do the task more quickly and better ourselves, but the consequences are that our subordinates never learn to do new things and that we run out of time whilst they run out of work.

  - Letting go of jobs that we like doing – this is called growing up.

  - Learning to trust and overcoming the fear of losing control.

  - The temptation to take back a job when a member of our team asks for help – employees are very good at upward delegation, so make sure the ball stays in their court; but always remember, you can delegate responsibility and authority but you cannot delegate accountability! For more on delegation see Chapter 3 of *Building A Winning Team*, the first book in this series.[5]

- **Use the 80:20 rule** – some things do need to be perfect, but, more often than not, 80 per cent is good enough. We all have a tendency to over-engineer and strive for perfection in all that we do. Ask yourself, 'Is it fit for purpose? Will it do the job?' If the answer to these questions is 'yes' then stop. Always have the Pareto Principle[6] in the back of your mind, that 20 per cent of the effort will give you 80 per cent of the benefit.

- **Eliminate wasted time:**

  - Plan your time. Schedule those important but not urgent tasks, but allow sufficient time to deal with all the day-to-day stuff that will land on your desk.

---

[5] Sutton, B. and Chatham, R. (2017) *Building A Winning Team*. Swindon: BCS.

[6] The Pareto Principle was coined by Joseph M. Juran and named after Vilfredo Pareto, an economist who discovered the rule and published his first paper on it in 1896.

- Handle items only once – as far as possible deal with each email and piece of paper then and there; you will only waste time having to reread them at a later date. If you cannot deal with it then and there, save future time by making quick notes in relation to the salient points and actions you need to take to jog your memory.

- Utilise dead time – use travelling time to catch up on reading material or to relax with a good book; waiting time can be used to catch up on your emails.

- Avoid procrastinating over those things that you don't feel like doing because they are difficult, unpleasant or uncomfortable. Do them first – you will be amazed at how much better you feel, and how much more productive you will be without the weight of an unpleasant task hanging over you.

- If you have a task that you are really struggling to get motivated to tackle try this 30-minute rule to help you get started. Start the task, but limit yourself to 30 minutes and then see how you feel. At worst, you will have broken the back of the task; at best, you may have achieved so much that you are motivated to continue to its completion.

- Be decisive – most of us waste plenty of time dithering over fairly trivial decisions; any decision is often better than no decision. If a course of action is taking you in the right direction then carry on; if it is not, remember you can always change course. Apply the 80:20 rule to information gathering; gather enough, rather than striving for all that is available.

- **Get organised:**
  - Be realistic about what you can achieve in any one day. Ensure you leave time to get yourself organised, delegate effectively, deal with the day-to-day stuff, eat and have a little 'me' time in order to switch off and relax. Allow for thinking time and remember that things often take longer than you think, so allow for this in your planning.

- Try to anticipate possible problems or difficulties in advance and also allow for these in your planning.

- Use a daily 'to do' list; do not include too many items and leave sufficient space for the unexpected. Maintain a second 'to do' list for longer-term tasks.

- Operate a one-place system – write everything down in one place, be it a tablet or notebook. If you need to refer back to who said what in a meeting or find a phone number, it will be there. It gets rid of the clutter and you will stop losing information.

- Chunk tasks – group small similar tasks together and do them as a batch, for example your email.

- Chop a large task down into smaller, more manageable pieces.

- Do not get side-tracked or distracted – if you think of something else you need to do whilst in the middle of another task, make a note so you will not forget it, but complete the task you are currently working on first.

- Do not leave things to the last minute.

- Develop a filing system that works for you and use it. You will need to allocate a little time each day to keep it under control.

- Make appointments with yourself in your diary. This is the personal time you need to get organised. It will encourage you to spend your time in the way you intended and also avoid other people filling the spaces in your diary for you.

- Finally, do not let other people's lack of planning throw you off course. As one fiery executive assistant we know would say: 'Your lack of planning doesn't make it my emergency!'

- **Learn how to say 'no'** – the vital thing to bear in mind is that you cannot possibly say 'yes' to everybody all of the time. It is far better to be honest and learn to say 'no' rather than 'maybe', 'if I can fit it in', 'possibly' or suchlike. Don't give people false hope. Be firm, be fair, be honest, be consistent and be polite. If it is your boss who is demanding your time, set out what you have to do and ask them to suggest a priority order, make sure they understand the potential consequences of any compromise they are asking you to make, write it down and get an email response from them that confirms that they set this priority.

- **Handling your email** – learn to use email appropriately and don't allow it to take over your life:

  - When messages are simple and straightforward, nothing can beat email; however, complex or ambiguous issues are always best dealt with face to face, or, at least, over Skype or the telephone. This will save time and also reduce the risk of your message being misconstrued. If using Skype and discussing a contentious issue, download Skype recorder and make a record of the conversation (you will need to inform all participants that you are recording the discussion). Email can then be used to confirm the outcome of your discussions.

  - Use the copy function ('cc') wisely and frugally and teach others, in particular your team members, to do the same.

  - Only mark something as urgent if it really is.

  - Make the subject line meaningful and flag emails for action in the subject line. Set an example and teach others to do the same.

  - If you do get copied in on things that you don't need to know about, either delete them without reading beyond the subject line or file them in a 'just in case' file. Do not feel obliged to read each and every email you receive.

  - Develop a folder system that works for you. When you have dealt with an email either file it or delete it – leave as little as possible in your inbox.

  - Develop the ability to skim read.

THINGS FOR YOU TO WORK ON NOW

Below are some questions that will help you build a picture of how you use your time and how you feel about the way you are performing at key points.

KEY QUESTIONS TO ASK YOURSELF

- Is how you spend your time controlled by you, or by events?

- If you feel that you are at the mercy of events, what steps can you take now to regain some control over your life?

- On a scale of 1 to 5, how organised do you currently feel? Write down specific examples of times when you have felt at a loss and also times when you have felt 'in the zone'. Try to identify the key things that made you feel this way in both cases.

- On a scale of 1 to 5, how efficient are you at completing tasks in a way that satisfies your customers and does not come back at you on a later date? Write down how you felt and what you were doing when you felt at your most efficient.

- What sort of things do you always put off doing? What is it about them that you don't like? What would have to change for you to start to feel differently?

- How effective do you feel you are at doing the right tasks?

- If you had more time, what would you do with it?

- How do you generally react to stress and pressure – does this make you thrive or does it paralyse you? Why do you feel this way?

Reflect on your answers to these questions and pick one aspect to work on over the next few weeks. To make this work, you need to think about your approach within the context of real tasks that you need to complete and that you find to be challenging in some way.

Below are some suggestions about things you can work on that may help you.

MINI EXERCISES YOU CAN TRY IMMEDIATELY

- Establish your priorities:
  - Summarise your purpose in one sentence – remember this is what you are employed for, not what you necessarily do.
  - Now consider how much of your time is spent fulfilling your purpose.
- Analyse how you spend your time:
  - Consider the calendar exercise you undertook at the beginning of the practical advice section. How have the percentages of time you spend in each category of tasks changed over the three-month period?
  - How do you feel about your progress?
  - Do some of the categories excite you more than others or do some confuse or concern you more than others?
  - What appears to be the source of your feelings about these tasks – is the focus one of skills or is it about attitudes or relationships?
- Now consider what you are going to do about it.

If you are inspired to find out more about any of the themes covered in this chapter we suggest that you start by reviewing the resources listed below.

FURTHER FOOD FOR THE CURIOUS

- Blanchard, K., Onken, W. and Burrows, H. (2011) *The One Minute Manager Meets The Monkey*. London: Harper Collins.

  - Short, simple and easy to relate to; the authors use a monkey analogy to highlight the issues of time management in relation to delegation.

- Covey, S.R. (2004) *The 7 Habits of Highly Effective People: powerful lessons in personal change*. London: Simon & Schuster.

  - More on the time management matrix which Covey popularised in 1996 in his book *First Things First*.

- Gallows, A. (2014) '4 things you thought were true about time management'. *Harvard Business Review*. Available from: https://hbr.org/2014/07/4-things-you-thought-were-true-about-time-management [29 November 2017].

  - A refreshing examination of some of the misconceptions about time management.

- Hallowell, E. (1999) 'The human moment at work'. *Harvard Business Review*, 77 (1). 58–66.

  - A very interesting article discussing the pros and cons of email communication, when to use it and when not to use it.

- Thomas, M. (2015) 'Time management training doesn't work'. *Harvard Business Review*. Available from: https://hbr.org/2015/04/time-management-training-doesnt-work [22 November 2017].

  - An interesting take on the impact of the modern world on our ability to manage our time.

6 KEEPING POSITIVE WHEN THINGS ARE GOING WRONG

The focus of this chapter is on your attitude towards life. Our attitude affects our relationships with others, our mental and physical reserves and our ability to handle the ups and downs of life in general and particularly in the face of adversity.

WHY IS THIS IMPORTANT?

We constantly have to deal with incompetence, stupidity, insensitivity, rudeness, indifference and those who simply can't be bothered; the list goes on and on. Events frequently conspire to mess up carefully laid plans: things don't turn up when they should do; a key player goes off sick at exactly the wrong time; your car won't start just as you are about to leave for a crucial meeting; your hard drive crashes when you have an important deadline. As they say, life can suck – bad things happen! When they do, keeping positive in the face of adversity can be challenging. In the right frame of mind, you may easily ride the waves. However, on another day it could be a very different story; when events conspire against you, they drain you of both your physical and mental energies.

> Some people deal with adversity more easily than others and some professions may be more challenging than others. Indeed, the IT profession is commonly cited as being one of the most stressful professions.

In search of the ultimate personality taxonomy, Goldberg used factor analysis to develop the renowned Five Factor Model (FFM) of personality traits.[1] One of these factors is **neuroticism**; it describes people with a 'tendency to experience unpleasant emotions easily, such as anger, anxiety, depression, and vulnerability'. It also concerns 'the degree of emotional stability and impulse control'[2] that a person may exhibit; it is connected to a pessimistic outlook on life and a predisposition towards stress.

Many IT people and many IT functions are perceived as being negative, pessimistic or adopting a victim mentality; they focus on why something is so difficult or expensive, that it will contravene standards, that it will compromise IT security and so on. Does IT therefore attract individuals who may score highly on the neuroticism scale? If this is the case it begs the question of whether it is the IT profession itself that is stressful or whether IT attracts the type of people that are more likely to suffer from stress.

Another personality trait held by many IT people is 'perfectionism'. Most IT people are very clever; they reach sound conclusions through logical data analysis – they know they are right. They also want to do things the right way, the best way and nothing less than perfect is good enough. When they do get it wrong, which everyone does from time to time, they have a tendency to beat themselves up, they may become grumpy or bad tempered, they may lash out at those closest to them.

You can learn to be more optimistic and you can learn to accept your fallibility.

---

[1] Goldberg, L.R. (1993) 'The structure of phenotypic personality traits'. *American Psychologist*, 48 (1). 26–34.

[2] Quote from http://wikivisually.com/wiki/Big_Five_personality_traits [22 November 2017].

THE IMPACT OF THE ISSUE

Everyone has to deal with problems, issues and things that just don't go right.

Letting things get to you is not good for you: your well-being, your productivity and your creativity will all suffer; your energy reserves will be depleted and your motivation will dwindle. Indeed, a report published in *Nature Neuroscience* substantiated that pessimism was not good for your health. A study of nearly 100,000 people showed the optimists among the group to have a lower risk of heart disease and lower death rate in comparison to the pessimists.[3]

> Just as enthusiasm is infectious, so negativism is contagious; a negative attitude will spread like wildfire and have a knock-on effect on all of those around you.

Think of the people you encounter in your life; some you may categorise as 'givers of energy' whilst others you may categorise as 'drainers of energy'.

In 1995, Daniel Goleman popularised the term 'emotional intelligence' in his book of the same name.[4] Basically, emotional intelligence is the ability to understand and deal with your emotions and those of people around you. Emotional intelligence is often measured as an emotional intelligence quotient or EQ for short. EQ describes an ability, capacity or skill to perceive, assess and manage the emotions of oneself, of others and of groups.

Being clever and having a high IQ will open doors to your chosen profession. However, once you are in that profession, EQ emerges as a much stronger predictor of who will be most successful; it is how you handle yourself in your relationships

---

[3] Sharot, T., Korn, C.W. and Dolan, R.J. (2011) 'How unrealistic optimism is maintained in the face of reality'. *Nature Neuroscience*, 14 (11). 1475–1479.

[4] Goleman, D. (1995) *Emotional Intelligence*. New York: Bantam Books.

that determines how well you do once you are in a given job. As a technician, EQ is a very important skill; however, as a team leader EQ is an absolutely essential skill.

As a team leader, you need the ability to get yourself out of a negative state, to ensure that your bad mood does not have a negative impact on your team and others around you. You need to have the discipline not to make hasty judgements in the heat of the moment or fire off that barbed email when provoked. You need to be able to rise above situations and not be tempted to 'cut off your nose to spite your face'. You need to allow others access to how you feel, so that they can understand where you are coming from and have trust and faith in your motives.

MAKING SENSE OF IT ALL

The real test of a positive nature comes in the face of adversity. When things start to go wrong, it is not so easy to stay positive. The test is how quickly you bounce back. You may find you have a moment or two when it all gets on top of you: you lose control, your composure slips and you feel the onset of despair. But when the moment is over, your fighting spirit should come back, your sense of humour can recover and you will start to see the funny side; you can make the best of the situation and take the proverbial bull by the horns. Consider the way Rupali dealt with her run of bad luck in the following story.

Rupali was going to a job interview for the position of development manager. It was a long and torturous journey and she ended up being nearly an hour late. Instead of making lame excuses about the traffic etc. she held her hands up and said: 'I'm really sorry. I've no excuse. It's all my fault – poor organisation and underestimating the time it would take. However, I am very talented in other areas.' The interview panel chuckled and asked for someone to get her a sandwich. Following the interview, she got the job.

When things are going wrong, some people try to ignore the situation. 'Sticking your head in the sand' and ignoring the problem is not going to help it go away. The longer problems remain unaddressed, the worse they usually become. Problems need to be embraced, not ignored. If handled properly, problems can be the catalyst that helps you to see differently and adopt new patterns of thinking. Problems are a powerful learning opportunity.

The question 'Did things go wrong, or just not as planned?' is always a good one to have at the back of your mind. When you double book yourself, your flight gets cancelled or a supplier delivers the wrong product, these are simply examples of **life** itself. You can't live a life in which everything goes according to plan. It's the ups and downs, the unexpected twists, the moments of serendipity that keep you on your toes and provide you with those special moments and instances of inspiration.

Perfection isn't living and living isn't perfection.

Life does not play out like some perfectly constructed script: it is about finding value in times of disillusionment, accepting that things won't always go as planned and using unexpected life experiences as opportunities; opportunities to get creative, to learn, to grow and to build bridges.

It is relatively easy to recover from minor glitches in your life. However, the challenge comes when something really bad happens, such as someone close to you becoming seriously ill or losing your job; these are the real tests that mark your ability to remain positive.

Having a positive attitude is vital for your well-being in life and for your success in business – as Zig Ziglar said, 'it is your attitude, not your aptitude, that determines your altitude'.[5]

---

[5] Ziglar, Z. (1975) *See You At The Top.* Gretna: Pelican Publishing.

Neurochemical expert Loretta Breuning believes that we humans can stop negative thought patterns by changing our brain chemistry.[6]

For many, looking for the worst in every situation is instinctive; indeed, your brain has evolved to scan for problems in order to help you avoid them and keep you safe. According to Breuning, you can transcend this natural negativity if you know how. The process involves consciously creating new thought habits and in so doing you will unconsciously be rewiring your brain. Instead of thinking 'this is going to be difficult because...', think 'this is an interesting puzzle to be solved'. Consider how the news media tend to put negative spins on situations whilst the advertising industry puts positive spins on things to encourage people to buy. Practise creating your own positive spin on situations. Breuning believes that this is habit-forming and, with a little practice each day for six weeks, you can rewire your brain and build new neural pathways that will help you to see the world in new and more positive ways.

Consider how in the following story Percy managed to put a positive spin on a potentially life-changing event.

At the beginning of the last recession Percy was made redundant from his position as IT controller for a regional building society. He hadn't been there long so only received two months' redundancy money. He had a large mortgage to pay and lived on his own. He first worked out how long he could survive without an income and calculated that if he was careful he could eke out his redundancy money for five months. He then mobilised his network to help in his quest for a new job – he found that half of the people he knew dropped him like a stone but the other half supported him both emotionally and practically. He found a pal in a similar situation and together they did lots of fun things together that cost no money – indeed

[6] Breuning, L.G. (2016) *The Science of Positivity: stop negative thought patterns by changing your brain chemistry.* Avon: Adams Media Corporation.

it became a game to see how little they could spend on a fun day out. He also took the opportunity to do all the things he had wanted to do in the past but had no time to do. Three months down the road he got a better job than he had previously, as a result of a recommendation from one of his networking contacts.

In this story, Percy did not just shift his attitude but also embedded a new set of observable behaviours that marked him out as imaginative, bold and self-motivated. These behaviours and the message they gave to the world about Percy's nature were instrumental in him finding a new job. Instead of being a victim, Percy took control of his own destiny and created a new range of possibilities for himself.

PRACTICAL ADVICE

There are many things you can do to help in staying positive and preventing those negative thoughts from taking root. Here are a few things you can do to help with staying positive when events conspire against you:

- **Do not be frightened or too proud to ask for help** – it is very easy to get so close to a problem that you can't see 'the wood for the trees'. In such cases, someone else may be able to take a different perspective, to see a way through that is not obvious to you; as they say, two heads are better than one.

- **Talk things through** – when you articulate your fears, worries or concerns out loud, often they don't sound so bad. When you get things off your chest, it can make it easier to move on. Psychologists point to the importance of 'change talk' – the idea that before people can move on, they have to articulate the things that are getting in their way.

- **When things go wrong (or not as planned), put the situation in perspective** by asking yourself the following questions:

  - Is this the end of the world?
  - Will the business fail?
  - Can I have another go?
  - Can it be mended?
  - Can I buy a new one?
  - How much will this matter in one, five or ten years' time?
  - What are the alternatives?
  - What lessons can I learn?
  - Will I be remembered for this in my dotage?

  These questions will help you to see that about 90 per cent of the things that you get worked up about are really rather trivial and, in the grand scheme of things, are not worth ruining your day over. Everyone has bad-hair days – do not blow them out of proportion. Get over it and move on; remember the saying: 'There is no point crying over spilt milk.'

- **Take time out** – forget about your problems for a day; just go out and do something fun. Go to a movie, go for a ride on your bike or have a game of golf, anything that is completely different, that you enjoy and that fully absorbs your attention. Re-address the problem another day when you are re-energised and in a better place.

- **Re-evaluate, not just the situation but also your outlook on the situation.** Instead of complaining about the plan that is not working out, make a new plan. Instead of griping about a procedure that failed to deliver the required outcome, analyse the reason why and develop a new and better procedure. Take action to create the best possible outcome, rather than stressing over outcomes that are unattainable. Life tends to be a self-fulfilling prophecy – positive thoughts produce positive outcomes and negative thoughts produce negative outcomes; you are either the master or the victim of your attitudes.

- **Focus on what you can control, or influence, rather than what you can't.** It is a pointless waste of energy and mental capacity fretting and worrying about things that you can't change; focus on what you can achieve, rather than what you can't. Don't let what you cannot do interfere with what you can do.

- **Try to see the funny side** – humour helps you cope in difficult times and lightens the mood. For example, a friend, who had recently been the victim of a robbery, on telling the story concluded with the quip, 'We finally got rid of that awful figurine that my aunt bought us.' Laughing also delivers positive physiological benefits; it reduces the stress hormone cortisol and it increases the infection-fighting lymphocytes in the bloodstream; it reduces the heart rate and blood pressure and relaxes the muscles in the chest and shoulders. So, there is a lot of truth in the saying 'laughter is the best medicine'.

- **Do not give up** – just because something went wrong once or failed, it is no reason to give up or not to try again. Remember Thomas Edison's famous saying, 'I did not fail: I just succeeded in finding 100 ways not to make a light bulb.' On a cautionary note, if you feel persistently sad, unmotivated, anxious, hopeless or fearful, it may be time to seek professional help.

Do not just wait for things to go wrong before you take action. The following everyday advice will help you to remain positive and look on the brighter side of life:

- **Plan your day** – this will help to improve your focus and prevent that overwhelmed feeling, provided that you are neither too ambitious nor too rigid. Ensure there is a little slack to enjoy some moments of relaxation, and delight in the serendipity of those chance encounters. Do not expect everything in life to go as planned; if you do, you will be quickly disappointed.

- **Don't strive for perfectionism in everything that you do** – adopt the 80:20 approach (see Chapter 5 on time management).

- **Look after your physical well-being** – exercise, eating well and getting enough sleep can all contribute to a positive attitude:

  - Exercise is good for both mind and body; those endorphins improve our mood and provide us with that feel-good factor.

  - Nutrition – as they say, 'An army marches on its stomach'; if you are not getting the right fuel in sufficient quantities, you will find it more difficult to find the energy to keep positive when things are going wrong. Indeed, the 'B' vitamins are particularly important for our mental well-being.

  - Sleep – you need sufficient sleep, and the right amount for you. If you have problems getting to sleep, try some relaxation techniques (see the next point) just before you go to bed.

  - Relaxation – everyone needs to unwind from their busy lives. Try listening to your favourite music, reading a novel, watching a TV soap, taking the dog for a walk, meditation or other relaxation techniques such as tai chi.

- **Inject some 'me' time into your life** – no matter who you are or what you do, everyone needs a little 'me' time each day to recharge those emotional batteries. This is one of the single most important things that you can do for yourself, so start today.

On a final note, ensure you live life to the full. Remember, your time on this planet is limited and finite, so don't waste it – life is not a dress rehearsal!

THINGS FOR YOU TO WORK ON NOW

Below are some questions that will help you understand how resilient you are when things go wrong. It is not enough to be technically capable and good at managing processes; business benefit is always delivered through people, and as a team leader you need to be able to support people as they wrestle with the ups and downs of life and the competing commitments that are thrown in their way.

KEY QUESTIONS TO ASK YOURSELF

- Am I a glass half full person or a glass half empty person?
- Am I a perfectionist?
- Do I let the little things that go wrong in my life get to me?
- How quickly do I bounce back when things do go wrong?
- What was my reaction, or my attitude, the last time something went wrong in my life?
- How prepared am I to ask for help?
- How willing am I to talk things through with others?
- What do I do to relax, to unwind?
- Do I get sufficient sleep and exercise?
- How good is my diet?
- Am I able to see the funny side of things?

Reflect on your answers to the above questions and pick one aspect to work on over the next few weeks. Think how you can weave this into both your work and personal life.

Below are some suggestions about things you can work on that will help you ride the roller coaster of life and stay positive.

MINI EXERCISES YOU CAN TRY IMMEDIATELY

- Practise a few relaxation techniques and see how they make you feel.

- Next time something goes wrong or not according to plan think of the positive spin that you could put on the situation.

- When overwhelmed by tasks or events, focus your efforts on the things you can do or change rather than dwelling on those you can't do or change.

- Plan a little 'me' time into your life. Start with small steps, e.g. aim to read a novel on that plane or train journey to work, rather than looking through your emails.

- For a period of two weeks, try to eat only healthy foods, minimise your caffeine and alcohol intake, get at least seven hours' sleep per night and take at least 20 minutes' exercise each day. Monitor how you feel and your ability to cope with life's ups and downs.

- Make a list of all the people you could turn to for emotional support, to unburden or to provide a little TLC.

If you are inspired to find out more about any of the themes covered in this chapter we suggest that you start by reviewing the resources listed below.

FURTHER FOOD FOR THE CURIOUS

- Breuning, L.G. (2016) *The Science of Positivity: stop negative thought patterns by changing your brain chemistry.* Avon: Adams Media Corporation.

- Through an understanding of the neurochemicals that drive our behaviour as mammals, the author suggests how we can harness our human brainpower to channel and control these mammalian urges in a positive way.

- Goldberg, L.R. (1993) 'The structure of phenotypic personality traits'. *American Psychologist*, 48 (1). 26–34.

  - A short paper describing the Big Five theory of personality traits, also known as the Five Factor Model.

- Goleman, D. (1995) *Emotional Intelligence*. New York: Bantam Books.

  - A comprehensive text on the subject of emotional intelligence; a little hard going, but with plenty of engaging examples.

- Sharot, T., Korn, C.W. and Dolan, R.J. (2011) 'How unrealistic optimism is maintained in the face of reality'. *Nature Neuroscience*, 14 (11). 1475–1479.

  - An insight into the neuroscience behind optimism and the health benefits of retaining a positive world view. The negative aspects of underestimating the risks are also discussed.

BIBLIOGRAPHY

Andersen, E. (2016) 'Managing yourself learning to learn: mental tools to help you master new skills'. *Harvard Business Review*, March. 98–101.

Baddeley, S. and James, K. (1987) 'Owl, fox, donkey, sheep: political skills for managers'. *Management Education and Development*, 18 (1). 3–19.

Blanchard, K., Onken, W. and Burrows, H. (2011) *The One Minute Manager Meets the Monkey*. London: Harper Collins.

Breuning, L.G. (2016) *The Science of Positivity: stop negative thought patterns by changing your brain chemistry*. Avon: Adams Media Corporation.

Chatham, R. (2015) *The Art of IT Management*. Swindon: BCS.

Clarke, A.C. (2000) *Profiles of the Future: an enquiry into the limits of the possible*. London: Indigo.

Covey, S.R. (2004) *The 7 Habits of Highly Effective People: powerful lessons in personal change*. London: Simon & Schuster.

Dillard, A. (2013) *The Writing Life*. New York: Harper Perennial.

Ericsson, K.A., Prietula, M.J. and Cokely, E.T. (2007) 'The making of an expert'. *Harvard Business Review*. Available from: https://hbr.org/2007/07/the-making-of-an-expert [20 November 2017].

Gallows, A. (2014) '4 things you thought were true about time management'. *Harvard Business Review*. Available from: https://hbr.org/2014/07/4-things-you-thought-were-true-about-time-management [29 November 2017].

Goldberg, L.R. (1993) 'The structure of phenotypic personality traits'. *American Psychologist*, 48 (1). 26–34.

Goleman, D. (1995) *Emotional Intelligence*. New York: Bantam Books.

Grote, D. (2016) 'Every manager needs to practice two types of coaching'. *Harvard Business Review*. Available from: https://hbr.org/2016/09/every-manager-needs-to-practice-two-types-of-coaching [22 November 2017].

Hallowell, E. (1999) 'The human moment at work'. *Harvard Business Review*, 77 (1). 58–66.

Hayashi, A. (2001) 'When to trust your gut'. *Harvard Business Review*, 79 (2). 59–65.

Kelly, T. and Kelly, D. (2012) 'Reclaim your creative confidence'. *Harvard Business Review*, 90 (12). 115–118.

Kelly, T. and Kelly, D. (2015) *Creative Confidence: unleashing the creative potential within us all*. London: William Collins.

Kolb, D.A. (1983) *Experiential Learning: experience as the source of learning and development*. London: Prentice Hall.

Leonard, D. and Straus, S. (1997) 'Putting your company's whole brain to work'. *Harvard Business Review*, 75 (4). 110–121.

Parkinson, C.N. (1955, 19 November) 'Parkinson's Law'. *The Economist*.

Portigal, S. (2012) *The Power of Bad Ideas*. Core 77. Available from: www.core77.com/posts/22446/the-power-of-bad-ideas-22446 [24 August 2017].

Schön, D.A. (1991) *The Reflective Practitioner: how professionals think in action*. Aldershot: Arena.

Senge, P.M. (1994) *The Fifth Discipline Fieldbook: strategies and tools for building a learning organization*. New York; London: Currency, Doubleday.

Sharot, T., Korn, C.W. and Dolan, R.J. (2011) 'How unrealistic optimism is maintained in the face of reality'. *Nature Neuroscience*, 14 (11). 1475–1479.

Sutton, B. and Chatham, R. (2017) *Building a Winning Team*. Swindon: BCS.

Taylor, D. (2002) *The Naked Leader*. Oxford: Capstone.

Thomas, M. (2015) 'Time management training doesn't work'. *Harvard Business Review*. Available from: https://hbr.org/2015/04/time-management-training-doesnt-work [22 November 2017].

Zenger, J. and Folkman, J. (2017) 'Why do so many managers avoid giving praise?' *Harvard Business Review*. Available from: https://hbr.org/2017/05/why-do-so-many-managers-avoid-giving-praise [29 November 2017].

Ziglar, Z. (1975) *See You At the Top*. Gretna: Pelican Publishing.

INDEX